Saying Yes to God

How to Keep in Step with the Spirit

Timothy C. Geoffrion

FOREWORD BY
M. Craig Barnes

 CASCADE *Books* · Eugene, Oregon

SAYING YES TO GOD
How to Keep in Step with the Spirit

Copyright © 2017 Timothy C. Geoffrion. All rights reserved. Except for brief quotations in critical publications or reviews, no part of this book may be reproduced in any manner without prior written permission from the publisher. Write: Permissions, Wipf and Stock Publishers, 199 W. 8th Ave., Suite 3, Eugene, OR 97401.

Cascade Books
An Imprint of Wipf and Stock Publishers
199 W. 8th Ave., Suite 3
Eugene, OR 97401

www.wipfandstock.com

PAPERBACK ISBN: 978-1-4982-9706-6
HARDCOVER ISBN: 978-1-4982-9708-0
EBOOK ISBN: 978-1-4982-9707-3

Cataloguing-in-Publication data:

Names: Geoffrion, Timothy C.

Title: Saying Yes to God : How to Keep in Step with the Spirit / Timothy C. Geoffrion

Description: Eugene, OR: Cascade Books, 2017 | Includes bibliographical references.

Identifiers: ISBN 978-1-4982-9706-6 (paperback) | ISBN 978-1-4982-9708-0 (hardcover) | ISBN 978-1-4982-9707-3 (ebook)

Subjects: LCSH: Self-help—spiritual. | Spiritual healing. | Spiritual life—Christianity. | I. Title

Classification: BT732.5 G50 2017 (print) | BT732.5 G50 (ebook)

Scripture quotations, unless otherwise noted, are from Holy Bible: New International Version, copyright © 1973, 1978, 1984. Used by permission of Zondervan Bible Publishers.

Scripture quotations noted NRSV are from the New Revised Standard Version of the Bible, © 1989, Division of Christian Education of the National Council of Churches of Christ in the United States of America, and are used by permission.

Manufactured in the U.S.A.   05/17/17

To my students, colleagues, and coaching clients,
who continually inspire me to say "yes" to God
more readily
with fewer excuses and reservations
with greater faith, sincerity, and dedication, and
with more love and genuine concern for others

Since we live by the Spirit, let us keep in step with the Spirit.

GALATIANS 5:25

Contents

Foreword

THERE ARE AN EXTRAORDINARY number of books on spirituality. After reading most of them, one is left just with a wistful sigh—"If only I had a connection to God like that." However, Dr. Geoffrion's book gives us something more. It makes a rare contribution to the field because it is deeply grounded in real life. He does not write theoretically or romantically about the spiritual life, but focuses on the actual work of the Holy Spirit among those who know all too well the dust and grit realities of daily life.

As he writes in his introduction, "This book is not at all about supernatural visions and ecstasy, mountaintop experiences or great spiritual triumphs. It's about learning how to hear and recognize the voice of the Spirit in the ordinary moments of daily life and to create a life that is one big 'yes' to God."

There is the real issue. How do we say yes to God when there are so many daily life issues pressing for our attention?

After thirty-five years of service as a pastor, who has been keenly attentive to what God is doing in the lives of my parishioners, the spirituality that pierces into the ordinary in ordinary ways is what fascinates me the most. Frankly, I think it is also what the Bible cares about the most.

Our Scriptures are filled with stories of the most miraculous, awe-inspiring events, but by the time we make it to the epistles of the New Testament it is clear that the miracles were never the point of God's sacred drama with us. Those were just a means of focusing our attention on the unpredictability of a world that has been pierced by the presence of the Holy. According to the apostles, the goal is to know how to live in holiness when there aren't miracles. That's why we're called to live by faith. And nothing is more faithful in the eyes of God than an ordinary, unspectacular life of communion with the Holy Spirit who binds us into the life of the beloved son, Jesus Christ.

Near the end of his letter to the church in Philippi, which was one of Paul's most mature end-of-life writings, he says:

> Finally, beloved, whatever is true, whatever is honorable, whatever is just, whatever is pure, whatever is pleasing, whatever is commendable, if there is any excellence and if there is anything worthy of praise, think about these things. Keep on doing the things you have learned and received and heard and seen in me, and the God of peace will be with you. (Philippians 4:8–9, NRSV)

The goal of spirituality is to live with "the God of peace," and according to this text the way to find God with us is to keep on doing what we know to be true, honorable, just, pure, pleasing, and commendable. In other words, do what we know to do.

After wasting far too many years of my life trying to pull off the spectacular, it has finally dawned on me that God loves routine acts of faithfulness. The spectacular and miraculous are up to divine intervention. Our calling is to keep wandering around the routine doing what we "have learned, and received, and heard. . . ." And it makes God so pleased to be with us along the way.

If spirituality cannot be found in the routine then it is just a distracting dream.

Who created routine? The God who made small things like electrons and huge things like planets spin around and around. Every year it's the same routine—winter, spring, summer, fall. It's creation's way of saying, "Praise God from whom all blessings flow."

I once had an electrocardiogram test for my heart. After the technician put a paddle on my heart, I soon was looking at the monitor that showed my heart valves opening and closing, and then immediately opening and closing again. Not only had I had never seen this before, I had never even thought about my heart valves. It occurred to me that the difference between my life and death was that these valves had to quietly and faithfully keep opening and closing. Then I began to think about their rhythm of praise to the creator of the heart.

Most of us don't wake up in the morning hoping our heart valves will keep working tirelessly. That's because we don't pay attention to the intricacies of the holy in our lives. But our hearts know how to praise God. They just keep doing what they know they were created to do.

G. K. Chesterton has written that the sun rises every morning not just because of the laws of nature, but because God commands it to get up there and do it again. Like a child, God squeals with delight to see the same things happen again and again, and exclaims every morning, "Do it again."

As the Apostle Paul instructs us, do it again. Do whatever is true, honorable, just, pure, pleasing, commendable. Do it again, and then again. And God will be with you.

So wake up choosing to be grateful for the day the Lord has made, and rejoice and be glad in it. Devote yourself to the holy words of the Bible before attending to the many other words you will encounter that day. Pray for your eyes to be open to the more subtle miracles you may encounter like the smile you find on a small Down syndrome child who greets you in the elevator. Pray also for your ears to be open to the still small voice of the Holy Spirit who will urge you to bend down and say hello to this precious creation of God. As the day filled with meaningless committee meetings, emails, traffic jams, and hard phone calls tempts you think this is all there is, pray for the eyes and ears to be attentive to the holy landscape in which your life is actually lived.

There is more than our hassled culture wants you to see. But learning to see also the holy is the point of spirituality.

This book will show you how.

M. Craig Barnes

President and Professor of Practical Theology
Princeton Theological Seminary

Preface

AFTER FOUR HARD YEARS in ministry, I left the pastorate discouraged and confused. I gave my heart and soul to the church, but I had become disillusioned. I didn't understand why there was such a gap between my expectations and what I was experiencing in real life. Why wasn't the church growing as I had hoped? Why was God letting so many people suffer and die—good people, followers of Christ, individuals we prayed for? Had I been too naïve in applying biblical teaching so literally? Perhaps if I understood the Bible better, I reasoned, maybe I would discover where I had gone wrong in my thinking and ministry.

I enrolled in a PhD program in Chicago looking for answers. I eagerly dove into the study of the Old and New Testaments. I hung on every word of my professors. I felt like I was getting filled up and coming alive again. Yet, I had no idea what God intended to teach me through the program, let alone where this journey was going to take me.

In the first semester, in an advanced level graduate course on the Apostle Paul, a single verse suddenly reoriented my thinking in a way that has radically altered my relationship to God and my approach to ministry and leadership ever since. As part of his lecture, one of my favorite professors, Dr. Edgar Krentz, read Paul's words recorded in his second letter to the Corinthians:

> [God] has made us competent as ministers of a new covenant—
> not of the letter but of the Spirit; for the letter kills, but the Spirit
> gives life (2 Cor 3:6).

I don't remember what point Dr. Krentz was making, but I knew in an instant I had just received the answer I was looking for—or at least what would lead me to so many answers over the coming years. The epiphany was not at all what I was expecting, but it was what I needed to hear: ". . . the letter kills, but the Spirit gives life."

I came to graduate school assuming that I needed more academic knowledge about the Bible to answer my questions. What I needed more was to learn how to relate to God in a more intimate way. I needed to learn how to listen better for the voice of the Spirit and how to let the Spirit guide my life and ministry on a day-to-day basis. I didn't just need more Bible study. I needed more of the Holy Spirit.

Since that moment of reorientation, almost thirty years ago now, I've been on a quest to understand what it means to experience the Spirit's leading and working in every possible aspect of my life and ministry. My study, writing, teaching, coaching, preaching, mixing with Buddhists and Muslims as well as Christians of every stripe, traveling to dozens of countries around the world, and now serving as a professor and spiritual coach in Myanmar and other countries in Asia, Europe, and Africa are all part of my insatiable desire to discover what is true about the Holy Spirit, and what difference the Spirit can make in the life of ordinary followers of Christ. I'm still on that journey, but what I've found so far has been life-changing for me and many others.

Saying Yes to God: How to Keep in Step with the Spirit is the latest fruit of my research, exploration, and personal experience related to the Holy Spirit. My quest for greater understanding has selfishly been for my own benefit. This book however is for my students, colleagues, coaching clients, and all those who, like me, want to know God more experientially, and want God's help to pass through the walls that have been holding them back in their lives. It's for those who are ready to give up trying to transform themselves, and want to learn how to be transformed by God. It's about how to draw better on the Holy Spirit in every way imaginable, in every aspect of their lives, for the sake of Christ and his kingdom. It's motivated by a desire for myself and for my brothers and sisters in Christ to be more of what Jesus envisioned for his followers—able to shine forth the light and love of Christ in a world full of suffering, injustice, and alienation.

Please note that the book may be read without reference to any of the footnotes. The notes are included for those who would like to find additional resources and nuances of meaning not addressed in the main text. On many occasions, I have included especially lengthy footnotes when I wanted to alert students and other interested readers to critical issues debated among scholars or to the views of well-known writers on Christian spirituality, and to clarify how my position coincides or differs from other important voices.

Acknowledgments

I AM DEEPLY GRATEFUL to all those who have contributed in a wide variety of ways to the creation, review, and completion of *Saying Yes to God*. In particular, I want to acknowledge the many contributions of my spiritual life coaching clients, students, colleagues, the board of directors of Faith, Hope, and Love Global Ministries, a dozen readers of the manuscript at various points along the way, and especially my wife.

Over the past ten years, my spiritual life coaching clients have proven to me that saying "yes" to God makes all the difference in the world to one's experience of God and to the quality of one's life. Their humility, openness, and responsiveness to the Holy Spirit have consistently led them to a place of love and peace in the presence of God, as well to new insight, clarity, and motivation. The principles and practices presented in this book are both biblically grounded and have grown out of my own personal experience, yet my coaching clients have shown me that these truths are not simply theoretical or idiosyncratic. They are applicable for any follower of Christ who wants to better know, love, and serve God. Many of my client's stories fill these pages as illustrations of this truth.

Along with coaching clients, two completely different groups of students were particularly helpful to me in refining and shaping the teaching in these chapters. The first was a small group of theological students at Myanmar Institute of Theology. The students met with me on Thursday afternoons, second semester, during the 2015–16 academic year. In our times together, we practiced the simplest versions of listening to God and asking God to speak a needed word into our lives. These students had never had any spiritual direction or instruction on how to listen to God on such a personal level. Our experience together showed me how easy it is for anyone to learn simple, but profound, spiritual practices—and to be well rewarded for doing so. Their testimonies affirm how responsive God is to those who are listening with the right kind of heart and mind-set.

A second group of students came from a Monday morning Bible study group at Christ Presbyterian Church (Edina, Minnesota). Each week, for four weeks, twenty-five to thirty adults met for two hours to work through the major teaching of this book. This group helped me to see the value of identifying and concretely naming the "walls" where each of us get stuck in our spiritual journey and relationship with God. Their engagement and responsiveness throughout our time together further strengthened my conviction that there is tremendous value of pushing hard on simple spiritual truths (such as listening to God, being humble and open, and loving others) to explore where, when, and why they become so difficult to live by in real life.

I'm also grateful for the inspiration and example of many pastors, faculty members, and other Christian leaders that I have met around the world, especially those who have had to make great sacrifices in order to serve Christ. In particular, I have been profoundly inspired and touched by the dedication of professors Lahpai Zau Lat, Edmund Za Bik, Samuel Ngun Ling, Cung Lian Hup, Maung Maung Yin, Eh Tar Gay, and many others, too many to try to name, who have served with me as fellow faculty members at Myanmar Institute of Theology (Yangon, Myanmar). They live their "yes" to God so concretely and extensively that I have come to see how provisional and self-serving my "yes" can be at times. Their examples have helped me to want to give more of myself in Christian service, and to do so with more humility. They've been showing me by their lives, usually without words, what it means to focus more on serving others and glorifying God than on serving myself and seeking my own glory.

The board of directors at Faith, Hope, and Love Global Ministries has been very encouraging over the long process of writing this book. Specifically, Peter Strommen, Thomas Erickson, and Michael Dircz have each in his own way affirmed the validity and value of the spiritual principles and practices that are presented in these chapters. More broadly, I am very grateful for their support and insistence that I not neglect writing in the midst of the many demands of teaching, coaching, and service abroad. Their commitment to me personally has been a great source of encouragement and practical help as well, as I seek to live out my own "yes" to God as fully as I can.

At critical points in the development of the book, a dozen different individuals read the manuscript and offered feedback, suggestions, and encouragement in multiple ways. Wherever I was able to incorporate the suggestions of these readers, I credit them with making the book better. Wherever I failed to adequately draw on their insights or address their concerns, I take full responsibility for this lack.

All of the readers were chosen because of their own track record for saying "yes" to Christ in their own personal lives, most of whom are ordained ministers, presidents of their congregations, leaders of Christian ministries, lay leaders, and/or actively serve as spiritual directors. In 2014, early on in the writing process, Judith Doré and Josias Hansen read the first draft of the introduction and chapter 1, when I first was starting to pull together the content and shape of the book. Each made observations that influenced the development of the book as a whole. At the end of 2015, Sylvia Bailey, David Carroll, Laura Crosby, Paul Harmon, Ed Sladek, David Stark, Eric Strobel, and Kim Thompson read the complete manuscript, giving me helpful feedback on what "worked" for them as well as what didn't work or what they felt was missing.

Early in 2016, Mark Burrows was particularly helpful. He generously read the entire manuscript and offered many penetrating comments and suggestions, not all of which I could act upon, but all of which were deeply appreciated. After one more round of editing, my beloved mother-in-law, Lucy Hartwell, proofread the text, word by word. In addition to the specific gift of finding typos and other grammatical issues, she offered sincere, personal words of encouragement, in the amazing way that only she can do, which I will always treasure.

Finally, I cannot express deeply enough my tremendous appreciation and gratitude to my wife, Jill. Time after time, when I needed wise counsel or a thumbs up to say "yes," she was the one who gave me what I needed. When I wanted to move too quickly or was headed in the wrong direction, Jill was the one who urged me to slow down or be more discerning. When I grew hesitant or unsure of myself, she reminded me of my gifts and calling. When being supportive meant great personal sacrifice for her, Jill usually still said "go." In all, Jill's love, support, encouragement, counsel, confidence, willingness to confront, prayers, personal example, and unbelievable dedication to me and our marriage have all contributed significantly to my ability to say "yes" to God in so many ways.

Introduction

IF YOU PICKED UP this book, I believe you care deeply about your relationship with God, and you want it to be better. You genuinely love God and are grateful for your blessings. You are trying to follow and serve Jesus Christ. You sincerely want to do God's will. Yet, at the same time, you are struggling, or simply longing for more in your relationship with God.

You may be yearning for some reassurance that you are on track as a follower of Christ. You may be hoping for some guidance or for fresh ideas to help you on your spiritual journey. You may sense that God is calling you to a deeper place, to a more spiritually dynamic life, or to do something special for God—and you want that, too. But something keeps getting in the way. Something is blocking you, hindering your ability to go forward, or holding you back.

Perhaps you feel conflicted about drawing closer to God. You may want to hear God's voice better, but you're afraid of what God might say to you if you listen carefully enough. Or perhaps, you may be discouraged from previous failures or frustrations. You may feel inadequate and reluctant to hear something you don't think you will be able to do. You might be living too much in a groove that you know and manage well, but which doesn't leave much space for God to speak into it. You might feel resistant, because you don't want to give up something you've been holding on to that doesn't fit with God's will for your life.

However, if you're feeling stymied or frustrated in your relationship with God, the outlook is better than you may think. The fact that you are struggling indicates that God is actively calling you to a deeper relationship, and that you care. Your growing dissatisfaction signifies that you're getting ready for change. If you weren't, you probably wouldn't even be aware of your limitations and wouldn't be struggling with where you're at

1

spiritually. No, the fact that you're reading this book suggests that you're already moving toward God or being drawn to God in some new way. But what does God have in mind?

Perhaps you are still having a hard time seeing and coming to grips with the fact that your relationship with God is still mostly about you. You want God's help to make your life better or more satisfying or happier. You think that if God would only help you more, then you'd have more of the life you're longing for. But again, it's the life *you* want, not necessarily the life God wants for you. Perhaps it's time to change the way you are looking at God or yourself, change the way you are trying to pursue your goals or find satisfaction in life, or change how you relate to God and go about trying to grow and serve.

The leading question of this book is not, "Is there hope for you and your relationship with God"? The answer to that is yes, absolutely! The questions needing to be answered are, "Are you truly willing to listen to God and cooperate with the Spirit's leading?" "Are you willing, in 'real time' today, to say 'yes' to God in whatever way the Spirit is leading you now?" "Are you willing to let go of your idea of what your life is or ought to be, and accept more fully God's calling for the life Christ wants for you?"

"Hitting a wall" in your spiritual life is a graphic and powerful image to describe what happens to everyone who takes his/her relationship with God seriously and desires to grow. It doesn't necessarily mean something is wrong. It may actually mean that you are finally ready for the next stage in your growth. When you hit a wall, you must face your inability to attain your goals or fulfill your desires in your way, on your terms, and in your own power. Yet, the emotional and intellectual impact of hitting the wall is a sign of hope, because it means you are now ready to listen to God in a new way and at a new depth.

Janet Hagberg and Bob Guelich in their book, *The Critical Journey,* talk about the wall as the place where we are "unmasked" and have to face what we have not been able to acknowledge about ourselves and our motivations up to that point. It's the place where we may have to face our own limitations and, frankly, our inability to be the person we wished to be. It's where our will meets God's will.[1] It's where we must "let go and let God," as many preachers are fond of saying, in a more profound and truly life-changing way than ever before. It's where we surrender.

1. Hagberg and Guelich, *The Critical Journey,* 175.

Hitting a wall, then, is actually a positive sign that you are growing (or poised to grow) in spite of the fact that it may feel as if you're coming apart. The wall prepares you to experience God and to develop in new ways, previously unavailable to you. There are many spiritual practices and resources you can draw on to help you at the wall, which will be discussed at length in this book; but in the end, God is the one who takes you through the walls in your life. Only God's Spirit can enable you to reach a more mature stage in your spiritual life. The walls in your life drive you to your knees where you must wait for God. There you pray, seeking, asking, and knocking on God's door, being purified and prepared for the Holy Spirit to take you somewhere you cannot reach on your own. This is your spiritual journey.

A Spirit-led life

The Apostle Paul taught that the Christian life is grounded in God the Father's immeasurable love for us, what Christ did for us on the cross, and the ongoing, active work of the Holy Spirit in our lives. Paul spoke often about the grace of God and our need to trust in Christ for our salvation. He also explained that, in practical terms, the Christian life depends on our relationship with the Holy Spirit. At one point, the Apostle Paul neatly summed up the critical role of the Spirit when he said to the Galatian Christians, "Since we live by the Spirit, let us keep in step with the Spirit" (Gal 5:25).

But what does it mean to live by the Spirit? What does it mean to keep in step with the Spirit? Do the two phrases mean the same thing? If they differ, how so?

Living by the Spirit

According to Scripture, there are many different ways in which we can or do live by the Spirit. Life in the Spirit begins with simply possessing God's life-giving breath, and thus applies to all human beings whether we recognize God's presence within us or not. However, the quality of how we experience the Spirit expands considerably when we enter a life-changing, personal relationship with Christ. In fact, the kind of experience with the Spirit is so qualitatively different from ordinary human life without Christ that we must consider this a kind of new life in the Spirit.

For the Christian, God's Spirit leads us to Jesus, gives us faith, and enables us to surrender our wills to God's will. Something happens inside of us that is like coming alive. We experience the forgiveness of sins. God takes away our guilt and shame. We become convinced that we truly belong to God and in the family of God. We come to love Jesus and want to follow him. We want to stop sinning, and we feel more strength and power to live for God, even if we still battle with stubborn sin throughout our spiritual journeys. All these experiences fit with what Jesus meant by being born again, or, being born of the Spirit (John 3:1–8). John explained that it is the Spirit of God that leads us to the truth about Jesus Christ, and that a true encounter with the love of God will transform us and enable us to become loving people in ways not possible beforehand (1 John 4).

As we mature in our relationship with Christ, we will experience more and more ways the Spirit breathes new life into our minds, relationships, and ways of being in the world. We will see God working through us to bless others and to enable us to contribute meaningfully in the church and in society. We will be better able to love God, ourselves, and others in life-giving ways. For all these reasons, we can say we are living by the Spirit, because God's presence in us and the Spirit's working in and through us gives us a life that was and is not possible otherwise.

More broadly, we can find in Scripture at least ten different ways the Spirit of God gives life to human beings, which would be particularly applicable to Christians. Though all of these references do not come from Paul's writings, together they represent a consistent New Testament perspective on how God works in human lives through the Spirit, and thus make up the theological world Paul was immersed in and contributed to. In bullet point fashion, we learn from Scripture that the Spirit . . .

1. Gives life to every human being (Gen 2:7; Ps 104:29–30; Acts 17:24-28).

2. Convicts of sin (John 16:7–11). The Spirit shows us our sin and convinces us it is wrong.

3. Guides us to truth and specifically enables us to have faith in Jesus (John 14:6; 16:13–15; Eph 2:8–9; 1 John 4:1–3).

4. Makes us spiritually alive in a renewed relationship with God (John 3:1–8, 16; 7:37–39; 20:19–23). That is, we are "born again."

5. Inspires a living hope and real joy, coupled with a deep love for Jesus (1 Pet 1:3–9).

6. Gives power to resist sin and to live at peace (Rom 8:1–6, 9; Gal 5:16).

7. Enables us to experience and exhibit "fruit" in our lives, which enable us to relate to others in more loving and godly ways (Gal 5:22–23; 2 Pet 1:2–3).

8. Helps us to pray in ways we could not do on our own (Rom 8:26–27; 1 Cor 14:2, 18; Eph 4:18).

9. Gifts and empowers us for Christian service to build up the body of Christ (1 Cor 12; Rom 12:3–8; 15:18–19; Eph 4:11–16).

10. Empowers us to fight and overcome evil (Eph 6:10–20, see especially vv. 17–18).

When Paul said, "we live by the Spirit" (Gal 5:25), he particularly was referencing the new life made possible since the coming of Christ and the outpouring of the Holy Spirit in the lives of believers in Christ.[2] Yet, and here is the critical assumption for this book, what is possible through the Spirit because we "live by the Spirit," isn't automatically the same as what we will experience in daily life. Though we truly live by the Spirit as believers in Christ in whom the Spirit is at work in life-giving ways, we must also learn how to get in step with the Spirit and then keep in step with the Spirit in order to keep growing and to live fruitful lives in Christ's service.

Keeping in step with the Spirit

So many of us know the "right answers" when it comes to following Christ and serving God, but we falter in our own efforts to practice what we preach at significant points. We may have experienced new life in the Spirit, and genuinely appreciate many ways we have experienced God touching, blessing, or working in our lives for good. Yet, at the same time, real gaps

2. According to Scripture, the Spirit was active in human beings in similar—albeit more limited—ways in Old Testament times. The Spirit would, on occasion, empower individuals in extraordinary ways and was a source of wisdom to all who would listen. Yet, the former ways of the Spirit are not foremost in Paul's mind in Galatians or in any of his writings. For Paul, Jesus' life, death, and resurrection along with the outpouring of the Holy Spirit are so significant that they have become the central pieces of his theology. Practically, since Pentecost, trusting in Christ and being led by the Spirit are now the key to a right relationship with God and to one's ability to please God and fulfill God's purposes for one's life. (See, e.g., Gal 3:1–5; Rom 8:1–8.) The ways God's Spirit has worked and works in the world among those who do not know or follow Jesus Christ is an important and relevant topic in pneumatology (the study of the Spirit), but outside the scope of this book. Here our focus is on the critical role of Holy Spirit for followers of Christ.

still exist at times between our ideology/theology/philosophy and how we conduct our lives, handle temptations, and respond to hard-to-love people. We're all trying, and most of us have seen fruit from God's grace and our efforts in many different aspects of our lives. Yet, at the same time, if we're honest, we will admit that we are also failing at key points, too. Either we just don't know what to do differently, or we lack the motivation, ability, or strength to do what Christ calls us to do.

This has been the story for Christians since the beginning. This is the story for every would-be follower of Jesus Christ. This human story explains why every writer in the New Testament not only announces God's wonderful love and grace extended to us through Christ, but also devotes significant space to overcoming ignorance, sinful desires, persistent resistance to God, and unhealthy, ingrained habits in everyday life. For practical Christian living, something more is needed than just faith or following the traditions we inherited. Something more is needed than having Christ in our hearts and possessing the Holy Spirit. Here is where keeping in step with the Spirit comes in.

When Paul said, "Since we live by the Spirit, let us keep in step with the Spirit," he was shifting from what God does for us to what we must do in response to the presence of Christ and the Spirit in our lives. The Spirit renews our hearts and minds, reveals truth to us, provides reliable guidance on our spiritual journey, empowers us to overcome our resistance to God, and corrects us when wander off the path, but usually doesn't force us to obey. That's something we must do. Though God is surely speaking to each one of us, we must listen for the Spirit's voice, and cooperate with his leading. Though the Spirit is the greatest power available to us, it is a resource we must draw on to benefit from it. Though the Spirit may even chase us and compel us at times, we still must say "yes" to God in order to keep in step with the Spirit.

Most, if not all, of the ways that we "keep in step with the Spirit" will flow from how we "live" by the Spirit. In other words, if you want to know how the Spirit might be leading you at any given moment, look back over the list of ten ways that we live by the Spirit (above). It is likely that the Spirit is prompting you in some way that fits one of his chief roles in your life.

The Spirit's prompting, stirring, enlivening, and empowering us provides the internal resources we need to live a Christ-centered, fruitful life, but we must draw on or respond to the Spirit's leading to make the called-for changes. We must take what we receive and then actively (re-) direct our attitudes, actions, and priorities in concrete ways that stem from the Spirit's life-giving presence in our lives. This may involve just remaining open to however the Spirit may choose to get our attention or speak to us, or it may require actively drawing on the Spirit's power and presence for whatever help we need.

In other words, keeping in step with the Spirit requires cultivating a lifestyle of listening regularly for the voice of the Spirit, and then staying ready to cooperate by following, obeying, and submitting our will to God's will in a hundred little ways every day. This is the meaning of Paul's imperative, and it is the only way any of us can grow spiritually and fulfill God's good purposes for our lives.

The life God is calling you to

The biblical vision for the ideal relationship with God is to know, love, and serve the God who loves us beyond what we can fully comprehend or imagine. To help us on our spiritual journey, we must draw on Scripture, put our trust in Jesus Christ, and be led by the Holy Spirit. Through Scripture we can expect God to most clearly speak to us. In the person of God's son, Jesus Christ, we will best know God's character and what true love is all about. By the Holy Spirit we will become convinced of the truth found in Jesus Christ and Scripture, and through the Spirit we can experience the love of God and transforming presence of Christ for everyday relationships and responsibilities.

As Spirit-led people, we will be fully engaged in life, inwardly living on our knees in humble gratitude for God's mercy and grace, and outwardly standing tall, drawing strength from Christ and God's call on our lives. We will move forward to serve confidently and fruitfully, not because of our self-generated worthiness or greatness, but because of the power of the Holy Spirit who ironically works in and through ordinary sinners saved by grace to bring good into the world. The Spirit helps us to believe that God's love and grace are so great that God can make something beautiful out of our lives, and can use us to bring love and beauty to others, no matter what our shortcomings or failures.

As Spirit-led people, we will increasingly see others through God's eyes, and develop a greater ability to love them in their imperfection. We will learn how to let go of so much judgment and condemnation, and will develop a greater ability to see and appreciate God's mark on each life. We will experience more compassion and empathy for those who suffer at the hands of others or because of forces beyond their control; and even for those who have brought suffering on themselves by their own poor choices and wrongdoing.

In the beginning, and in the end, the life God is calling us to is steeped in love. We are God's children created from love and for love. In Jesus Christ's life and death, we see the extent of God's love, and we benefit from Christ's sacrificial service in life-changing ways. Through the working of the Holy Spirit, we can experience this divine love internally and in many practical ways through other people and in a wide variety of circumstances. God's love continues to flow to others through us, as we learn to move out of our self-centeredness to reach out to those around us, through our smiles, generosity, kindness, service, understanding, forgiveness, and in a host of other ways as well.

The challenge for so many of us is to slow down enough and to quiet ourselves adequately so that we may connect to the divine source of love (the Holy Spirit)—to experience real inner change and to be freed from our own self-serving instincts and habits to become a conduit of that love. We develop spiritual practices to help us listen better to whatever the Spirit may be saying to us from moment to moment. Then, as we hear God's voice, we must draw on that same divine source of love to find the wisdom, will, strength, and courage to follow the promptings.

How you get there

In this book, you will read about many ways to grow in your relationship with God and about what it looks and feels like to keep in step with the Spirit as a way of life. But be prepared for some surprises. Expect to learn more about yourself and to hear the Spirit's voice revealing truth that you uniquely need to hear. For example, as we listen better to the voice of the Holy Spirit, we typically discover that it is not the failure of God to communicate that keeps us from growing or knowing how God is leading. Rather, it is often we who are getting in the way.

Sometimes we are too passive; often too controlling; sometimes too fearful; other times too stubborn. Some of us are too cerebral, and we make life too complicated or get paralyzed by our need to understand everything before we can simply follow the prompting of the Spirit. Others of us are driven by our feelings so much that we too easily lose our balance or get off track, or we draw the wrong conclusions from what we experience. Too often, we don't hear, let alone respond appropriately to, the Spirit, because, down deep, we don't want to hear what God wants to say, or we are not disciplined enough to step back from our experience long enough to hear something that may not fit with our preconceived notions. We may be too attached to our own will or desires. We may want to hold on to our anger or resentment. We may love our way of life or our way of seeing things more than we love Christ. Whatever the exact reason, when it comes down to the real barrier to our growth, it's often that we simply don't want to change.

For others of us, trust is the key issue. We've been burned, disappointed, hurt, or confused. We trusted God and things didn't turn out the way we thought they would or should. Now we may be gun shy, and afraid to trust again. Or, we just can't truly believe that God's way is better than our way. Intellectually, we can easily affirm that God's way is best, and we might even pray that God's will be done. Yet, at our core, we don't trust God enough to let go of our way in favor of following however the Spirit might be leading.

The good news is that the solution to most if not all these issues and challenges is much closer and more accessible than you might think. To create a better relationship with God, the most important thing is to look to God rather than yourself for the way forward. Rather than focus on learning how to not be something (i.e., being overly concerned about being too this, or too that) or how to do more of something (e.g., have more faith, be more faithful), the key to keeping in step with the Holy Spirit is actually quite simple. It's about reaching out to God, trusting that God will come near to you in response (Jas 4:8; Heb 4:16), and even trusting that God is the one drawing you in the first place. It's about submitting to Christ again, especially in those areas where he has been marginalized or ignored, and asking for the grace to live first and foremost for Christ and his kingdom in every relationship and role that you have.

In other words, perhaps the best thing you can do right now in your spiritual life is to make it less complicated. Set aside all mental or emotional blocks that you've constructed. Take a few deep breaths—or maybe many deep breaths. Relax. Remember that your God is a loving Father, who wants to give you good gifts.[3] Turn your eyes upon Jesus, as the old hymn wisely advises. Open yourself to listen for the voice of the Spirit in a fresh way.

3. See Luke 11:13; Jas 1:17.

Let the Holy Spirit lead you back to the foundation of your relationship with God—to God's unconditional love, mercy, and grace; to Christ's sacrificial love for you and the world; and to the cleansing, renewing breezes the Holy Spirit has breathed into your soul in the past. Instead of working harder and harder to try to fix yourself and then take action, draw close to God so that the Holy Spirit may pour out God's love into your heart in a fresh way. Ask the Holy Spirit to do in you what you cannot do for yourself.

The place to begin is where you would begin with anyone with whom you would like a better relationship. You engage the other person and focus on drawing closer to one another. You bring to mind why this relationship is important to you, and why you would like it to be better. You open yourself up to the other person. You commit yourself to being transparent and as honest as you know how to be. You are willing to talk about the problems, concerns, or questions you have that are interfering with the relationship. You make yourself vulnerable by expressing the longing of your heart, along with your hopes and dreams. If it is not too awkward or uncomfortable, you think and talk about love—how you would like to be loved by the other person and how you would like to express your love in return.

The Christian life requires learning how to say "yes" to God in everyday life, especially in situations that matter most but may be overwhelming or seemingly too difficult to handle. The more we learn how to recognize and rely upon the leading of the Spirit in all relationships and circumstances, the more we can relax and yet stay focused on what matters most in the moment. We will feel freer, more whole, and greater joy and peace. Ultimately, our ability to love others effectively and serve Christ fruitfully will grow and grow.

How this book intends to be helpful

Helping you to better listen to and flow with the Holy Spirit is what this book is all about.

As such, it is a practical resource on how to get and keep in step with the Spirit. It is designed to make life-changing spiritual practices simple and accessible to both theologically and non-theologically trained individuals. It's for all those who want to grow personally, relationally, and spiritually; and for those who want to follow a Christian path to do so. The book is especially geared for those who have faced their own limitations and even personal failures, and are looking for fresh insight and practical suggestions for how to move forward from wherever they find themselves, how to get unstuck, and how to climb out of the holes they may have created for themselves. It's a book both for those who feel eager and ready to grow in new ways and for those who find themselves at a wall, who may even feel that they are out of steam, ability, or insight to know how to take the next step.

This book is not at all about supernatural visions and ecstasy, mountaintop experiences or great spiritual triumphs. It's about learning how to hear and recognize the voice of the Spirit in the ordinary moments of daily life and to create a life that is one big "yes" to God. The spiritual practices discussed in each chapter will help you to see better how God is at work in your life and how to respond to God's call more freely and fully. *Saying Yes to God*, then, focuses on helping you to go with the flow of the Spirit as a way of life, as you both humbly but confidently take responsibility for your life and rely on the grace and working of God at the same time. All the stories in these chapters are taken from real life, and are drawn from spiritual life coaching clients and from others I have counseled or coached over the years. With their permission, I share them to illustrate how listening to and cooperating with the Spirit works in everyday life.

Saying Yes to God: How to Keep in Step with the Spirit is the third in a series of books designed to help readers draw on the presence and power of the Holy Spirit in practical ways. The first one, *The Spirit-Led Leader: Nine Leadership Practices and Soul Principles,* focused on how to develop a more vital relationship with God and how to serve more effectively as a Spirit-led leader in a position of authority.

The second book, *One Step at a Time: A Pilgrim's Guide to Spirit-Led Living,* grew out of my family's experience walking 500 miles across northern Spain on the *Camino,* also known as *El Camino de Santiago de Compostela* and the Way of Saint James. The goal of that book was to help Christians better understand and navigate their spiritual journey. In it, I identify various steps an earnest Christian pilgrim needs to take to move from a vague Spirit-led stirring to real spiritual growth and personal transformation. *One Step at a Time* also includes several chapters on how one might develop a deeper and more profound, personal relationship with each member of the Trinity, God the Father, Jesus Christ, and the Holy Spirit.

This third book goes even deeper into the practical dynamics of listening to, relying on, and cooperating with the Holy Spirit on a day-to-day basis. It is designed to help mature and maturing Christians better recognize the voice of God and grow in their ability to follow the Spirit's leading in wide-ranging ways. It offers fresh insight to break through barriers and personal limitations in knowing, loving, and serving God. The ultimate purpose is to help believers live fuller and more fruitful Christ-centered, Spirit-led lives.

Saying "yes" to God

The book is divided into two sections, and each chapter offers specific action steps that you can take to get or keep in step with the Spirit. The first part focuses on the critical importance of learning how to listen well to God and how to cooperate better with the Spirit's prompting. The second part focuses on how to keep in step with the Spirit, especially in the face of the many distractions, discouragements, and difficulties that threaten to derail your commitment, faith, and motivation.

Part I: Getting in Step with the Spirit

1. Listen and cooperate. A Spirit-led life in its most basic form is simply listening to God and cooperating with however the Spirit may lead. We should expect that the Spirit of God is speaking to each of us frequently, usually inaudibly and often quite subtly, but nonetheless prompting us in ways that do not come from our own thinking or planning, and that sometimes even go contrary to our will or desires. Our part is to listen and respond appropriately to whatever we hear—not by blindly following every idea that comes to mind, but by engaging the thought or feeling with a cooperative attitude, ultimately choosing a course of action that best fits with the flow of the Spirit and will of God as best as we can discern it. (*Chapter 1.*)

2. Be humble and open. Practically, in order to become more comfortable and confident as a Spirit-led follower of Christ, we need to put ourselves in a frame of mind and heart that is receptive to the Spirit. We need to humble ourselves before God. We must approach God from a place of honesty and openness to whatever the Spirit may want to communicate to us, trusting that God will respond to us in loving ways that fit with God's good purposes for our lives. (*Chapter 2.*)

3. Be discerning. No matter how inspired we may feel, Spirit-led living is not just proceeding on the basis of our feelings, hunches, and hopes; it often requires thoughtful reflection and choosing to exercise our freedom to make decisions according to godly values and priorities. A discernment process normally involves wrestling with what we are hearing and seeing, reflecting on how we are living our lives, examining our motives, and finally making hard choices where we are genuinely free to choose among different options. By exploring issues, studying Scripture, clarifying our values and priorities, dialoguing with others, including those who see things differently, we grow in our ability to make wise, Spirit-led decisions and serve Christ as adults. (*Chapter 3.*)

4. Commit to "yes." When the Spirit starts prodding and stirring something with us, we need to be responsive. We should take the prompting seriously, listen long enough to know what it is about, and determine what cooperation will look like. Once we are clear about the calling, we will not have rest until we put our "yes" into motion. "Yes" will look different depending on the prompting and circumstances, but it always involves commitment and action. (*Chapter 4.*)

5. Join the sacred love flow. At the core, Spirit-led living is all about love. As followers of Christ, we are called to love others deeply, something made possible because God pours out God's love into our hearts through the Holy Spirit. Whatever the Spirit says to you, and however the Spirit may lead you, you can be sure it has something to do with love. The more we focus on living fully, loving deeply, and giving freely, as Christ defines these priorities, the more we will be in sync with how the Spirit thinks and is moving within us. (*Chapter 5.*)

6. Don't quit on love. Sometimes, loving others can be really tough. In fact, at times it may seem impossible. When we've been hurt, our relationship with someone has broken down, or there is a long history of tension and conflict, we may neither feel love nor feel any capacity to forgive or act in loving ways. Yet, it is precisely at such times that Spirit-led love is most needed. No matter how hard someone may be to love, we are commanded by Christ to love them anyway, and it is the Holy Spirit who can enable us to do so. (*Chapter 6.*)

Part II: Keeping in Step with the Spirit

7. Overcome evil with good. As the journey continues, we usually discover that, at times, keeping in step with the Spirit gets harder, not
easier. We may feel overwhelmed by the needs we perceive, and the
extent of the evil and suffering in the world. Yet, at the same time, we
will increasingly feel compelled to do something beyond whatever we
have dreamed of doing before. In the face of great need, we must not
focus on what we can't do, but on the good we can do—or, even more
important, on what God can do through us. (*Chapter 7.*)

8. Take sin and grace seriously. The greatest impediments to Spirit-led
living are not the forces we meet that work against us, our lack of
resources, or obstacles in our way. The biggest threat to our ability to
fulfill our callings is within us—those attitudes, actions, and life habits
that block or run contrary to a Christ-centered, Spirit-led life of love.
In other words, to use traditional biblical language, sin in our lives
holds us back and undermines our best efforts to reflect the light and
love of Christ. Our only hope is to draw on God's grace and the Spirit's
power in greater ways than ever before. We must ask God to help us
face the truth about the darkness in our lives, and for power to come
to grips with the moral, spiritual, and deeply personal issues that are
alienating us from God and others. No matter how extensive our sins,
painful our suffering, complicated our questions, or gnawing our unfulfilled desires, the way forward is by drawing closer to the Spirit, not
running away from God. We must take sin seriously, and take God's
grace even more seriously, in order to break through the barriers and
stay in the sacred love flow. (*Chapter 8.*)

9. Be God-confident. Once we become more confident and comfortable
in getting in step with the Spirit and living in the sacred love flow, we
must also do all we can to keep in step with the Spirit as the challenges
and opportunities to serve Christ keep growing. At its core, keeping
in step with the Spirit requires maintaining confidence in God on a
day-to-day basis. We must rely on God's work in our lives, pouring
love into our hearts, giving us hope, breathing new life into our souls,
and working through us in ways that fit with God's purposes. We must
trust that the Spirit will guide us, even if we are unsure at times about
the signals and signs we are perceiving. We must order our lives on
the basis of our faith and grow in our ability to see God at work in the

world in the midst of chaos and evil. We must not shrink back as the call gets tougher or scarier. We must be bold and keep going with a self-confidence that is built upon God-confidence. (*Chapter 9.*)

10. Keep the faith. As we take seriously the call to listen to the Spirit as a way of life, and to make love our highest priority, our faith will be tested. Spirit-led living will take us out on the proverbial limb to places we thought we would never go, or could go; but love has compelled us to go there. The scarier it becomes, or the more we feel threatened in some way, the more we might find ourselves hesitating and asking questions. Is it safe? Will God come through? Is it worth the risk?

    To continue on this Spirit-led path, in the face of our hesitation or fears, we will need to come to grips with whatever unresolved questions we may have about God. We may find ourselves suddenly wondering about God's goodness, reliability, and involvement in the world and in our lives. Our suffering or the suffering of others may be stirring up feelings of anger, horror, or fear. We will need to find, or firm up, our faith, trusting that God is for us and is at work in our lives for good, even if we're not always sure how. (*Chapter 10.*)

11. Ask for the help you need. The deeper we delve, the further we go, the more we step out in faith to serve Christ in concrete ways, the more we realize that we simply cannot fulfill God's will for our lives in our own strength or by our own wisdom. We may have believed this intellectually for years, but experience has convinced us of our need for God's grace and power along the way. So, we must ask for the help we need—be it for wisdom, understanding, courage, the ability to repent, strength, comfort in suffering, provision, or anything else. We must learn to pray as we breathe—all the time, for everything, in every situation, drawing on the Spirit to be able to do whatever we are being called to do. We must take initiative to draw upon whatever resources are available to us. (*Chapter 11.*)

12. Live your "yes." Finally, saying "yes" to God is not something we do once, or occasionally. Saying "yes" to God is a way of life. It's a response of the heart, a commitment of the will, an attitude of the mind, and gut conviction that together keep us spiritually alive and always ready to move forward as the Spirit so leads. Our goal is always to reach a point where being a Christ-centered, Spirit-led servant of God defines who we are as well as our vocation—not only in our minds, but increasingly in every aspect of our lives. (*Chapter 12.*)

It's all about love

In the end, developing a better, personal relationship with God as a Christ-centered, Spirit-led servant of God often comes down to living in the sacred love flow more and more. This is true for God's calling on an individual as well as for God's calling for a church or any Christian community. Love is God's primary way to relate to the world and primary way to transform it. Love starts with God, flows to the world in general, expresses itself preeminently in the life and death of Jesus Christ, fills the heart of each believer in particular, and then shines through us to one another. Those who are led by the Spirit bask in God's love and mercy, and serve as conduits of God's love to others. Spiritual growth is a matter of knowing God's love more deeply and extending God's love more fully and expansively to others in every possible circumstance of our lives.

Participating in the sacred love flow was John's definition of being a Christian (1 John 4:7–8). It's where we start when the Spirit leads us to faith in Jesus, and the way of love marks out for us the path forward. We are born from God's love, we are reborn through love, and we are called to live lives of love, more and more over time. None of us does this perfectly, and all of us get tripped up by our own selfishness and unredeemed aspects of our personalities and ways of being in the world at times, yet God's love is the beginning and end of our callings.

The Apostle Paul's prayer for the Ephesian Christians expresses well this vision of a Christ-centered, Spirit-led relationship with God that is rooted in love and serves as the indispensable foundation for becoming more and more godly—literally, full of God, and thus full of love. His prayer is my prayer for you as you read this book:

> I pray that out of [the Father's] glorious riches he may strengthen you with power through his Spirit in your inner being, so that Christ may dwell in your hearts through faith. And I pray that you, being rooted and established in love, may have power, together with all the saints, to grasp how wide and long and high and deep is the love of Christ, and to know this love that surpasses knowledge—that you may be filled to the measure of all the fullness of God.
>
> EPHESIANS 3:16–19

16

PART I

Getting in Step with the Spirit

1

Listen and Cooperate

And I will ask the Father, and he will give you another Coun-
selor to be with you forever—the Spirit of truth. The world
cannot accept him, because it neither sees him nor knows him.
But you know him, for he lives with you and will be in you.

JOHN 14:16–17

WHAT HAS GOD BEEN saying to you lately?

Do you have some nagging thought or feeling that just doesn't go away? Do you get the impression that God may be trying to get a message to you, but you're not sure what it is, or can't bring yourself to believe it—or accept it?

Or, on the other hand, are you frustrated that God doesn't seem to be speaking much to you at all? You've been praying, asking, waiting, but getting nothing back. Nothing. You would really like some guidance, but your prayers don't seem to produce anything.

You believe, you may even teach and lead others, but you're struggling with how to lead yourself spiritually. You'd like more help from God, but either you're not getting it or you don't know how to recognize what God's saying to you.

What is the way forward?

Mike's frustration

Pastor Mike[1] loved his church and the people there, but he was unhappy. As a junior member on a large staff, he often felt under-utilized and stymied. There was so much he wanted to do and accomplish, but he just wasn't able to get there. He kept getting assignments that took his time and energy, but he wasn't satisfied either with what he was doing or the results. When was he going to be able to really do what he was made to do? When was the church going to set him free to run with his dreams and passions? When was he going to be fully appreciated and entrusted with more responsibility?

By the time Mike entered coaching he was frustrated and discouraged. Why wasn't God answering his prayers? Why wasn't God changing his boss and opening doors for him? He was starting to question himself, his calling, and even his confidence in God. His attitude was deteriorating. He was getting more and more angry.

However, through the coaching process, Mike finally realized that others were not the source of his unhappiness. He was. His inability to hear the voice of God was not due to God's silence but to his resistance to acknowledging what he already knew down deep. The truth was, the Spirit *was* speaking to him. He was feeling nudges, but since they didn't line up with what he wanted, he ignored or misinterpreted the signals. The Spirit was preparing Mike to leave that large, affluent suburban church to take a position elsewhere where he could better pursue the dreams God had given him for inner-city ministry. Yet, until Mike was willing to face his attachment to his current church and his anxiety over making the big change, he was going to stay stuck.

A simple path: listening and cooperating

In its most basic form, our ability to "keep in step with the Spirit" (Gal 5:25) comes down to listening for the small voice of God within us and cooperating with the Spirit's promptings, as a way of life. This is what Spirit-led

---

1. I am sharing Mike's story, including direct quotes, with his permission. All the individuals mentioned in this book and their stories (if told in a form potentially recognizable to others) are used with permission. When a name appears in quotation marks the first time I mention it, it means it has been changed to preserve the privacy of the individual. Where I have been given explicit permission to share someone's name and story, I use that person's real name without ever using quotation marks around it.

living is all about, and it applies to every possible aspect of our lives, every day. It's not magical and rarely astounding. It's usually straightforward, often subtle, and extremely practical. Still, keeping in step with the Spirit has to be learned—not because it's complicated or reserved for the highly educated or gifted few, but because it is so natural and simple that some of us can miss the Spirit's leading while looking for something more dramatic. We lack confidence in the little promptings of God so we flounder looking for something else that may never come.

Others of us can miss the Spirit's leading because down deep we actually don't want it. Listening to what threatens us can be very painful or frightening. Either we don't want to face some unflattering deficiency in our lives, or we can't bear the thought of having to make changes we don't want to make. As a result, our minds may work over time to discount or question what we're feeling and sensing. Something or someone is telling us to open our eyes, to listen to our heart, or to change our behavior; but frankly, we don't want to. In discerning God's leading, careful deliberations about important matters are usually wise and needed, but for some of us, we develop a complicated mental process that is little more than a mask for our resistance, stubbornness, or outright rebellion.

In the end, such resistance is exhausting and counterproductive. So much energy is chewed up trying to justify ourselves or to prove why our way of thinking or doing something is actually right or better than whatever the voice emerging from within us is proposing. Our fear of what God might ask us to do blocks our ability and willingness to listen. No matter what the source of the voice, if the idea is a good one, and we resist, we're usually sorry. We wind up restless, frustrated, disappointed, and generally unhappy. If instead we listen to the voice with an open mind and heart, the result is entirely different. We will usually be led to whatever truth we need to hear in the process of listening carefully.

Listening is at the heart of a living relationship with God

Whether we are adept at hearing God's voice or not, the teaching of the Bible makes clear that we are all called to learn to listen for the voice of God and to be ready to respond appropriately. Over and over again in literally hundreds of verses in both the Hebrew Scriptures and the New Testament, believers are told either explicitly or implicitly to "hear" or "listen" to the words of God. Usually the call signals that the prophet or teacher is going to reveal the will of God or give instructions to believers that must be followed.

As one important example, the Hebrew verb *shema* ("to hear") appears in one of the most significant Old Testament texts, traditionally known as the Shema[2]: "Hear, O Israel: The LORD our God, the LORD is one. Love the LORD your God with all your heart and with all your soul and with all your strength" (Deut 6:4–5). These verses are foundational in the Judeo-Christian tradition, because they affirm Israel's belief in one God and introduce the commandment to love God with all one's being, a directive Jesus later called the greatest commandment of all.[3] The points of significance here are, first, that the content of the teaching includes the call to "hear" the Word of God and is not simply an introduction to what follows. To listen to the voice of God is constitutive of a right relationship with God. Then, as a second and equally important point, when one listens to God the most important message one will ever hear will have to do with love. As Spirit-led followers of Christ, we, too, can expect that over and over again the Spirit will lead us to express love for God or love for others. Our primary job is to listen and to follow the love promptings.

Listening to God means listening to Jesus and the Holy Spirit

Starting with the New Testament, Jesus becomes the one we are to listen to. Jesus stands at the center of God's revelation of himself and of all that is good, right, and true. At Jesus' baptism, God the Father says, "This is my Son, whom I have chosen; *listen* to him" (Luke 9:35, italics added).

According to the Gospel of John, Jesus spoke of himself as both the good shepherd and the gate, whose sheep "listen to his voice" (10:3). Jesus adds that there are sheep that are not from the same pen who also "listen to my voice" (10:16). When confronted by Pontius Pilate, Jesus declared, "Everyone on the side of truth listens to me" (18:37).

2. Deut 6:4; the verb is also found in Deuteronomy at 4:1; 5:1; 6:3 and 9:1.

3. In its biblical context, the Shema sets the stage for the Ten Commandments in Deuteronomy. In Hebrew tradition ever since, the Shema has also formed an important part of the Jewish evening and morning prayer, as part of a confession of faith. Jesus' teaching on the primacy of love can be found in all of the Gospels: Matt 22:37; Mark 12:30; Luke 10:27. Cf. other New Testament teaching on the importance of love as the primary marker of those who know God and follow Christ, e.g., John 13:34; 1 John 4:21.

After Jesus' death and resurrection, the Holy Spirit takes his place as the day to day guide for believers. Before his death, Jesus spoke of the coming Spirit of truth, who would "teach [them] all things and remind [them] of everything I [Jesus] have said to [them]" (14:17, 26). The implication was that it would be very important for Jesus' disciples to be listening for the voice of the Spirit, who would be sent by God to tell them what they needed to hear.

At the end of his long upper room discourse, Jesus returns to the subject of the Spirit and its[4] important role in the lives of his disciples:

> I have much more to say to you, more than you can now bear. *But when he, the Spirit of truth, comes, he will guide you into all truth.* He will not speak on his own; he will speak only what he hears, and he will tell you what is yet to come. He will bring glory to me by taking from what is mine and making it known to you. All that belongs to the Father is mine. That is why I said the Spirit will take from what is mine and make it known to you. (John 16:12–15, italics added)

Jesus was not saying that the Spirit's role was to guide all followers of all times into new truth, but rather was to help Jesus' disciples to understand what they could not accept at the time of his earthly ministry, namely who he was and the suffering he had to endure on behalf of the human race. Thus, on one hand, we should not think that the Spirit will be the source of revealing all truth on all subjects on an ongoing basis. Jesus' promise of the Spirit, as found in John 16, was primarily for his disciples,

---

4. In the Greek, the word for Spirit/spirit is *pneuma*, a neuter noun. Thus, apart from any theological considerations, it would be appropriate to translate pronouns for Spirit in non-gendered or impersonal terms, such as "it" or "its," unless the context clearly suggests otherwise. Further, to avoid what feminist critics rightly view as undue "masculinization" of God, I minimize using masculine pronouns for God and retain the grammatically correct neuter pronouns for Spirit, with the exception of whenever I quote recognized translations of the Bible that retain the traditional masculine pronouns. However, when *pneuma* refers to the Holy Spirit, there are legitimate reasons why English translations typically translate corresponding pronouns and the subjects of third person singular verbs referring to the Spirit in masculine terms, i.e., as "he," "his," or "him." First, Paul equates the Spirit of Christ with the Holy Spirit, a fact that argues for the personal nature of the Spirit (as opposed to an "it") and perhaps even the appropriateness of the masculine pronoun, though we should not think of spirit/Spirit as masculine or feminine. Second, classic Christian Trinitarian theology has traditionally identified the Spirit as one of the three persons of the Trinity and thus not an impersonal force or "it." Third, occasionally, the biblical writer will use a masculine pronoun in reference to the Spirit (e.g., John 16:12).

who would need help to make sense of Jesus' crucifixion and glorification.[5] At the same time, the fact that the Spirit was God's tool for opening their minds, refreshing their memories, and zeroing in on truth for the disciples indicates that these are the kinds of things the Spirit does—not just for the apostles but in anyone with whom the Spirit has contact. Bottom line, when the Spirit speaks, we should expect to hear important truths pertaining to our relationship with God, to the person and work of Christ, and to what it means to follow Christ.

Listening to God today

The key to recognizing the voice of the Spirit, then, is to notice when truth is revealed to us in whatever form it comes, and cooperating means accepting the truth that we hear and acting accordingly. The Spirit usually doesn't speak to us in an audible voice, though many people have had that extraordinary experience. "Connie," for example, was a very successful businesswoman, doing many important and interesting things globally, traveling 85,000 miles per year to Europe and throughout the United States. She loved her job and had no interest in doing anything else. Until, that is, she heard God's voice saying, "Go home." Up to that point, she had been feeling a growing sense of discomfort over the amount of travel required of her. The Holy Spirit had been nudging her, telling her that she was needed at home. But the tipping point came when, on a business trip one night in a hotel room, she heard an audible voice literally telling her to go home. This message confirmed to her that the Holy Spirit had been trying to lead her to make a change, and specifically that she should quit her job and stay close to her family. That experience began months of agony for her as she wrestled with God's will for her life. To quit or not to quit? She certainly did not wish to leave her highly rewarding job, but she wanted to obey God.

Fortunately, her husband and close friends helped in her discernment process, as the right kind of friends often can. One in particular pointed out how rare it is for anyone to hear God speak to them audibly (for a sane person, that is), and thus she really should listen. Finally, she let go. She yielded. She received from her friends what she needed in order to be able to say "yes" to God. Soon thereafter, when the opportunity to give her notice suddenly presented itself, she took it.

5. Levison, *Inspired*, 150.

Her boss was shocked. Her husband fell to his knees overwhelmed with joy and gratitude. Her kids were thrilled. Connie felt dazed. She wasn't sure what hit her or what she was going to do around the house all the time, in spite of the fact that she had teenagers and a husband who were happy she would be there. There must be some reason God called her home, but what was it?

Six months later the answer came. Her mother had a serious stroke, and now needs her help daily. Had she kept working, Connie could have quit when her mother had a stroke; but, as she puts it, she might have resented her mother for it. This way, by listening to the Spirit and cooperating in a timely manner, she was not only there and available to care for her mother when she most needed her, but she felt peaceful and even grateful to be able to do so.

You may never have an experience of hearing an audible voice as Connie did or of God speaking to you in dreams or visions as many people experience, but you can certainly expect to hear God's quiet voice in your mind over and over again throughout your lifetime. This voice provides wisdom, direction, caution, inspiration, reassurance, comfort, and any number of other needed messages to help guide us on our Spirit-led journey. Indeed, as Christian philosopher, university professor, and author, the late Dallas Willard insisted, "from the individual's [various] experiences of hearing God, the 'still, small voice' has a vastly greater role than anything else."[6]

Something gets our attention, someone communicates a message we need to hear, or we feel some inner prompting to move in one direction or another. The mode varies depending on the person, the circumstances, and the need, but whatever the manner of the communication, the common denominator will be truth. Every word from the Holy Spirit will have the ring of truth to it—or if it doesn't at first, it will over time.

Since the birth of the church, followers of Christ have recognized and experienced truth in the reading, preaching, and teaching of Scripture, through which God's Spirit speaks. We listen for the truth found in words written by Old Testament prophets and New Testament apostles; and we also rely on the Spirit to convince us of the truth that we hear. Paul explained to the Corinthians that their faith was not the result of clever speech or argumentation, but came the from the demonstration of the Spirit and power. He may have been referring in part to signs and wonders he performed, but

6. Willard, *Hearing God*, 115.

he was also talking about their being convinced internally by the Spirit. In Paul's context, philosophers of his day and Jewish religious authorities, who relied on self-evident truths, their traditions, or their own rational abilities to determine truth, were rejecting the Gospel as foolishness. Yet, those who experienced the Spirit in the process of hearing the Gospel often became believers and followers of Jesus.[7] Accordingly, when Paul wrote to the Christians in Thessalonica, he reminded them, "Our message of the gospel came to you not in word only, but also in power and in the Holy Spirit and with full conviction" (1 Thess 1:10).

Thus, amid all the competing voices, ideologies, religious notions, surging emotions, and other challenges to knowing God and perceiving God's will, we should expect that God will, in various ways, penetrate the fog and bring truth to us. God may speak to us through dreams, visions, or an audible voice, but most often the Spirit speaks to us through Scripture and whispers truth in our minds in the midst of daily life in order to lead us to Christ, to help us to grow and mature, and to lead us along the spiritual journey.

We should expect the Spirit to speak to us through Scripture both to convince us of general truth and to convict us of particular applications of general truth. Both are important because, in Scripture, we are given theological and ethical teaching applicable to all followers of Christ that provide the intellectual basis for our faith and discipleship. At the same time, the Spirit will often use Scripture to address very personal, specific issues in our lives as well. In the second letter to Timothy, we read how extensive and valuable the role of Scripture can be in the spiritual formation of believers:

> . . . from infancy you have known the holy Scriptures, which are able to make you wise for salvation through faith in Christ Jesus. All Scripture is God-breathed and is useful for teaching, rebuking, correcting and training in righteousness, so that the [person] of God may be thoroughly equipped for every good work. (2 Timothy 3:15–17)

Clearly, there is not just one spiritual purpose for Scripture, just as there is not just one way to access its depth and richness. Bible study, preaching, meditation on Scripture, and devotional readings of Scripture (such as *lectio divina*),[8] among other such spiritual practices, complement

---

7. See 1 Cor 2:4–14.

8. See Smith, *The Word is Very Near You*, for a helpful guide among numerous resources available for praying with Scripture.

one another, all of which are beneficial for the maturing Christian. Each one provides a different vehicle to listen for the voice of the Spirit, and each one contributes something different to our spiritual growth.

Then, in addition to how the Spirit speaks through Scripture, we must learn to rely on the small voice of the Spirit in the midst of daily life. It is through prayer and life circumstances that we develop a deep, personal relationship with God in which the Spirit helps us apply Scriptural truths day to day. An intimate relationship with God, marked by ongoing communion with God in all settings and by listening for the voice of the Spirit amid daily life, is what Brother Lawrence practiced so extensively and led to what is now known as "the practice of the presence of God."[9]

But, once again, reading Scripture and filling our lives with spiritual practices are of no value if we are just doing them out of obligation or because we want to be or appear to be religious. For an authentic, life-changing relationship of God to develop, we need to be listening, too.

What Mike experienced in listening

Spiritual life coaching has taught me how transformative prayer can be when we take extended time to listen to God with one another. Over and over again, I've seen the Spirit reveal important, personal truths that wind up being just what the other person needs to see or hear. Sometimes it is a powerful image. Other times it is a word of reassurance. Sometimes, a meaningful verse from Scripture will come to mind, or God will bring clarity about what is most needed at this moment in time.

When Mike was willing to let go of his anxiety and really listen to what the Spirit had to say he quickly discovered that he had nothing to be afraid of. In fact, the Spirit wanted to affirm his gifts and abilities in ways that gave him greater confidence to set out in a new direction. He began to find new motivation and power to be the person God had called him to be, even in the midst of an increasingly unsatisfying work context. As time went on, he noticed he was changing. Ahead of one session he wrote, "I think there has been a shift in how I'm living and how I perceive myself. I find myself being the person I want to be rather than just wishing to be that person. [For example] when I wake up and haven't allowed time to be with God and to pray, I miss that time and find time later in the day."

9. Lawrence, *The Practice of the Presence of God*.

In one session, using a guided prayer format I have found to be very helpful, I urged Mike to consciously release his hurts, frustrations, and tension. I asked him to rest in God's affirmation of him as God's child, gifted to serve Christ. Then, after a few moments, I suggested he ask the Spirit to show him what he needed to see about his situation, and about what steps he needed to take next.

This could have been a scary prayer for Mike, but he chose to trust God with his fears. When he opened his eyes after a few minutes of silence in the presence of God, a warm smile spread across his face. His eyes lit up. "What did you hear, Mike?" I eagerly inquired. Without any hesitation he replied, "I experienced an overwhelming feeling of hopefulness. I heard God say to me, "You've got a bright future. I want to use your giftedness for me and my kingdom.""

Two years later . . .

Recently, when Mike wrote to me to give me permission to use his story, he wanted to let me know again how rewarding it's been for him to have listened to the Spirit and made the change he felt led to make. He explained, "People often ask me if I'm happy in my new position and church. I usually respond that their question doesn't get at my motivation for leaving [because] it was really a question of seeking fulfillment rather than happiness. These last two years have been the hardest, most fulfilling two years of my life. I have been stretched and broken more times that I can count but I'm more alive than ever before and seeing God show up in ways I couldn't have imagined before."

What might the Spirit say to you?

From the perspective of faith, whenever the voice we hear is the voice of truth, we can receive it as from the Holy Spirit. The Spirit will always say something to us that fits with God's good purposes for our lives. The message will be supportable by Scripture in most cases, either by explicit teaching or by general principles. Our spiritual mentors, mature friends, and godly counselors will be able to help us determine if what we heard is a reliable, trustworthy word.

For many of us, one of the clearest examples of how the Spirit speaks to us is when we hear or feel the call to come to God. The Spirit wakes us up, creates a longing in our hearts, and draws us to God so that we want to be in relationship with God. The voice or calling may be so strong that we feel compelled to listen and respond to the calling.

This kind of experience often marks the conscious beginning of our spiritual journey, such as when we first put our faith in Christ. The inner clarity may come from reading Scripture, a sermon, the words of another Christian, an ah-ha moment of realization, or a voice in our heads. We may become convinced that we cannot do enough good to earn God's approval or save ourselves, and the prompting inside of us points us to the love of God as our only hope. Or, we may simply want a relationship with our Creator and feel compelled to throw ourselves at the feet of God.

In my case, I was smoking a cigarette on the porch of my parents' home on a rainy Sunday evening when I was a young teenager. For some reason I told God that if he made it stop raining I would go to church. Before I knew what was happening, a voice in my head as clear as one I might hear if someone were speaking to me audibly said, "Who are you to give conditions to the almighty God?" In that moment, I knew only one response was appropriate. I threw down my cigarette, walked to the church in the rain (which never stopped), and sat down in the back row of the sanctuary just in time for the start of the sermon. By the end, I knew without a doubt that the pastor's invitation to commit one's life to Christ was meant for me. I bent the knees of my heart and put my life and trust in Christ that night, and a new relationship with God was born.

For many of us, conversion to faith in God and Christ marks the beginning or at least a significant turning point in our spiritual journey. Regardless of what our experience was exactly, whether we consciously submitted our will to God's, accepted God's forgiveness in way that felt real and freeing, put our trust in Jesus as our Savior, embraced God's love for ourselves personally, yielded to a sudden overwhelming sense of the Spirit's presence, or something else, a conversion experience usually means we've experienced firsthand what truly listening and responding to God is all about. Since that pivotal point, we have learned that we need to keep listening to and responding to the moving of the Holy Spirit as way of life, even if we struggle at times to hear or know how to interpret the voice of God.

To grow in our ability to hear and respond to the Spirit, we need to develop our ability to look for and recognize how God is communicating to us. The Spirit may remind us of some truth in Scripture that we need to remember. We may have a deep sense of knowing what is the right thing to do in a certain situation, perhaps as a word of wisdom or simply as new clarity about what would be loving, generous, kind, and helpful.

How have you experienced God speaking to you over the years? What kinds of messages have you received in the past that might help you as you are struggling to hear God's voice now? Perhaps God wants to assure you of God's great love for you. The Spirit may be calling you to spend more time with God or to use your time in prayer and devotion differently. The Spirit may want to tell you that you need to forgive someone, or that you need to forgive yourself.

Perhaps the Spirit wants to show you something God wants you to do. The Spirit may tell you about some changes that are needed in your life. You may need to change your attitude about someone or something. The Spirit may nudge you to reach out to show Christ's love to someone who is lonely or hurting. There are many things that the Spirit might say to you. What's most important is that you are listening, and that you stay ready to respond appropriately.

What is an appropriate response?

More than anything else, what God wants from us is our "yes."

When God told Abraham to leave Haran to travel to an unknown land that God would later show him, Abraham got up and left (Gen 12:1-4). When Joseph was alerted to the will of God in various dreams, he responded by believing that God would bring about what was revealed and by courageously speaking up (Gen 37—41). In fact, nearly every hero in the Bible, or simply anyone held up as an example of faith and faithfulness, did something—not to earn salvation, but as an appropriate response to God's grace and call on his/her life.

The Bible also contains stories about individuals who initially resist God's call, but who eventually listen, accept, and wind up serving in significant ways. Moses, for example tried to get out of his calling to deliver his people from slavery by not believing God really could use someone like him. Moses said to God, "Who am I, that I should go to Pharaoh and bring the Israelites out of Egypt?" (Exod 3:11). After firing off several more questions, perhaps hoping to avoid this divine assignment, Moses finally resorted to pointing out his inadequacy—his poor verbal skills (Exod 4:10). Finally, in spite of his questions, hesitancies, and fears, Moses accepted

God's call, and you know the rest of the story—Israel escaped from Egypt and was taken to the promised land.

In the New Testament, we find Jesus saying "yes" to God, the disciples and apostles saying "yes" to Jesus, and the early church saying "yes" to the Holy Spirit in many different ways. As was true in the Old Testament, the New Testament also portrays believers as responding to God's call on their life by listening and cooperating, obeying, serving, and giving themselves to fulfill God's will, sometimes at great personal sacrifice, sometimes even death. Mary, for example, is one of the best known models of someone who submitted fully to God's will, when she famously said to the angel who told her that she would bear God's son out of wedlock, "I am the Lord's servant. . . . May it be to me as you have said" (Luke 1:28).

What's new in the New Testament is that we find that all believers are promised the Spirit, filled with the Spirit, empowered by the Spirit, gifted by the Spirit, and led by the Spirit, who helps us to say "yes" to God.[10] It is the same Holy Spirit that has been at work in human lives since the beginning of time, including in the lives of Old Testament believers, but since Pentecost, believers are given the Spirit in ways that New Testament writers distinguish from what they had prior to Christ, and in a form that is distinguished from the divine life-force (spirit) in all human beings.[11] Now,

10. While there are many examples in the Old Testament of the Spirit of God empowering, bestowing special skills on, and giving wisdom to individuals, in the New Testament the Holy Spirit now functions in every believer's life in ways that are fundamental to their salvation, relationship with God, and ability to serve God as part of the body of Christ. For a verse by verse exposition of how Paul portrays the role of the Holy Spirit in the lives of believers, see Fee, *God's Empowering Presence*. In an appendix, Fee also briefly surveys "The Spirit in the Old Testament" (904–910; cf. Levison, *Inspired*). Professor Jack Levison has done some of the most extensive research on the Holy Spirit in recent years, writing both on an academic level and for general readers. His careful exegetical work offers a well-conceived, intriguing alternative to a more traditional understanding of the relationship of the Holy Spirit to human existence and to one's relationship to God. In short, Levison emphasizes the presence of the Spirit in all human life, and posits that what Christians experience through the Holy Spirit is an increased amount of what all humans already have. (See below for more detail on Levison's views.) While I appreciate his appropriate emphasis on the continuity between the Old Testament and New Testament believers' experiences of the Holy Spirit, and his careful work to show how the wisdom of the Holy Spirit is indeed available to all human beings, too much emphasis on continuity can obscure the clear distinction the Apostle Paul made between those who are in Christ and those who are not, in terms of how the former have received the Spirit in extraordinary and life-changing ways.

11. Jesus said the Spirit would be given to those who ask (Luke 11:13), i.e., the Spirit was something other than what they already possessed. In Acts, we're told that Peter

the Holy Spirit's presence and working are indistinguishable from the faith and faithfulness of believers. A "yes" to God is now both an outflow of God's grace in an individual's life (a humble submission to God enabled by God's grace but experienced as an act of surrender to God's will) and an intentional, willing participation in a life in the Spirit (again, a response enabled by God's grace but experienced as an act of the will and disciplined decision to focus on the mind of the Spirit rather than on the mind of the sinful nature). While Old Testament believers also depended on God's forgiveness, cleansing, and empowerment to live faithfully, New Testament believers have been given the Holy Spirit in keeping with Jeremiah's prophecy of a new covenant (Jer 31:31–34). With the coming of Christ and the outpouring of the Holy Spirit on all believers, God is no longer seen as an external resource but a constant, internal presence that offers personal intimacy with God and real transformation.[12] As a result, a "yes" to God

came to realize that God accepted Gentile believers because God "gave the Holy Spirit to them," (Acts 15:8), i.e., what God gave them was additional to the breath of God within them that gave them physical life. The Spirit has been given to believers as a guarantee of their salvation (2 Cor 1:22; Eph 1:14). Believers in Christ have "received" the Spirit who reveals the gifts of God to them (1 Cor 2:12). Each follower of Christ is given a "manifestation of the Spirit" to build up the body of Christ (1 Cor 12:7). God "sent the Spirit of his Son into our hearts, the Spirit who calls out, 'Abba, Father'" (Gal 4:6). The Spirit, which believers receive as a result of their Christian experience, is a "spirit of adoption," who prays with and for them (Rom 8:15, NRSV). And critically, Paul taught, only the Holy Spirit can enable believers in Jesus Christ to escape the power of sin (Rom 8:1–6), something made possible because "the Spirit of God lives in [those who are in Christ]," implying that there are those who do not have the Spirit of God (or Christ) living in them (Rom 8:9–11).

12. Cf. Levison, whose careful and extensive research on the nature of the human spirit and its relation to God's spirit, as portrayed in canonical Scripture as well as other ancient religious and philosophical writings, rightly identifies the continuity between the Holy Spirit and the human (God-given) spirit, but leaves one unable, in my opinion, to distinguish adequately between Creator and creature, or between what all humans have in common (apart from Christ and faith) and what Christians have when they receive the Holy Spirit. For example, Levison argues that the full biblical canon offers compelling evidence that "affirms that people who are other than Christian can experience the spirit of God within them from birth as a source of wisdom, knowledge, skill, and holiness" (Levison, Inspired, 66). While this observation rings true in part, it does not do justice to the tone, teaching, and intention of New Testament writers (Luke and Paul especially) who differentiate between the experience and capacity of ordinary human beings and that of believers in Christ who are endowed with the Spirit by "receiving" from God what they did not already have (e.g., Acts 10:44–47). As another example, Levison does not capitalize "holy spirit," because, in his opinion, what Christians have traditionally called the Holy Spirit is the same "spirit-breath" that is operative in all human beings. (Biblical writers use the same Hebrew and Greek words, ruach and pneuma, respectively, when

now requires not only submission to the will of God (Old Testament standard), but also both a personal relationship with God in Christ and a life of cooperating with the flow of the Spirit on a daily basis (New Testament).

Jesus, of course, modeled one big Spirit-led "Yes!" in his devotion to serving God's purposes, culminating in choosing to endure brutal treatment and martyrdom on the cross. At one point he summed up his self-understanding by declaring, "The Son of Man did not come to be served, but to serve, and to give his life a ransom for many" (Mark 10:45). Jesus' famous words in the garden of Gethsemane, hours before his crucifixion, further demonstrate the extent of his "yes" to God, when he said, "Father, if you are willing, take this cup from me; yet not my will, but yours be done" (Luke 22:42). Yet his response to God was not only a submission of his will. It was also a yielding to and dependency on the Spirit's activity in his life. As Luke's gospel makes particularly clear, from his conception to his validation at his baptism, his miracles, and many other aspects of ministry, Jesus' "yes" to God is virtually inseparable from the working, leading, empowering, and filling of the Holy Spirit.[13] His life and response to God's call was thus a precursor to the Spirit-led life all his followers would eventually be called to embrace.

In perhaps his most radical demand on his disciples, Jesus taught that discipleship meant giving one's whole self in response to his call on their lives. We read in the Gospel of Mark:

> Then he called the crowd to him along with his disciples and said: "If anyone would come after me, he must deny himself and take up his cross and follow me. For whoever wants to save his life will lose it, but whoever loses his life for me and for the gospel will save it." (Mark 8:34–35)

---

speaking of God's Spirit or the human spirit [*Inspired,* 162]). Again, while this observation is meaningful, it fails to fully reflect the general portrayal of the Spirit of God as something that is given to believers, i.e., is additional to the spirit God has already placed within every human being. See Fee for a detailed discussion of the ambiguities and issues involved in translating *pneuma* in Paul (*God's Empowering Presence,* 14–28). At the same time, while maintaining a proper distinction between the Holy Spirit and the spirit of life that God gives to all humans, Fee rightly observes that, for Paul, "the believer's spirit is the place where, by means of God's own Spirit, the human and divine interface in the believer's life" (*God's Empowering Presence,* 25).

13. See Luke 1:35; 2:27; 3:16, 22; 4:1, 14–21; 10:21.

According to tradition, ten of the eleven original disciples (excluding Judas, the one who betrayed him) were eventually martyred as a result of their faith and devotion to Christ.

The Apostle Paul both modeled this kind of radical commitment and taught others to do the same. In his own life, his "yes" to God meant obeying Christ's call to bring the Gospel to the Gentiles at great personal sacrifice. At the same time, true to Jesus' example and the New Testament emphasis on the Spirit-led life, he consistently indicated that God's working in and through him was the power behind his ability both to carry out his mission and be fruitful in it.[14] His willingness to suffer great hardships, including imprisonment, beatings, deprivation, and ultimately martyrdom further demonstrated the extent of his "yes," as well as his belief that God was powerfully working in his suffering for good and enabling him to endure all things.[15] Over time, he continually prayed and sought God's guidance and provision as he sought to live out his "yes." His response was consistent: he kept listening and cooperating with however the Spirit led him all along the way.[16]

In his teaching, Paul insisted that all who are recipients of the grace of God should respond with their own Spirit-led "yes" to God. For example, in moving from eleven chapters on the grace of God generously given to undeserving sinners, Paul begins the ethical portion of his letter to the Romans by saying, "Therefore, I urge you, brothers [and sisters], in view of God's mercy, to offer your bodies as living sacrifices, holy and pleasing to God—this is your spiritual act of worship" (Rom 12:1).

Listening to the Spirit of God is only the first step in a Spirit-led life. Responding with our "yes" is what completes the interaction and brings our spiritual life alive. God's grace always precedes our "yes," but hearing and doing go together, as James points out with particularly pointedness: "Be doers of the word, and not merely hearers who deceive themselves" (Jas 1:22, NRSV). The moment of truth for the Spirit-led Christian will not be, "Will I agree with the Spirit in this situation or not?" but, "Will I act on what I'm hearing?"

---

14. See Acts 13:46–48; 15:17; 22:21; 26:15–19; Rom 15:15–19; Gal 1:14–17; 2:7–9; cf. 2 Tim 4:17.

15. See 2 Cor 1:8–11; 4:7–11; Phil 4:12–13.

16. E.g., see Acts 13:1–4; 16:6–10.

Conclusion

As followers of Christ, we can expect the Holy Spirit to be working in our lives and leading us in meaningful ways all the time. Our job is to learn how to listen better and to be ready to respond appropriately, even if or especially when we are unsure what the Spirit is saying or if God is speaking to us at all.

The Spirit's goal is to bring truth to us in ways that draw us closer to God, enlighten our understanding, and actually transform us. The Spirit opens our eyes to see the truth about Christ, shows us how to follow Christ and live out the truths of Scripture in our everyday life, and actually makes us more and more like Christ—or, as Paul put it, "conform[s us] to the likeness of [God's] son" over time.[17] Scripture is often at the center of this transformative process by which we are conformed to the image of Christ.[18] By continuing to pray with Scripture, the message we hear often develops and expands as we listen for how to apply what we've heard in any number of practical, day-to-day situations. And by our repeated encounters with God through Scripture and in prayer, we are often changed.

The simple path of listening and cooperating calls for reaching out to God from our heart and mind, and making the effort to notice when God is reaching out to us. We will seek out the Holy Spirit as a constant companion, who will show us what we need to see and will inform our thinking and perceptions of what is happening around us. We will ask the Spirit to empower us to act and to respond to others and circumstances in ways that fit with God's good purposes for us and them.

In other words, listening and cooperating becomes a way of life as we move through each day in close fellowship with God. This is probably what Paul meant when he said we should "pray continually" (1 Thess 5:17)—not that we are always on our knees talking to God, but that we are in continual communion and conversation with God's Spirit no matter what we are doing. Beyond asking God for something or to do something, we will keep opening ourselves to the Spirit and seeking to draw near to God, mentally and emotionally. God becomes the primary influence in our consciousness. We will have one eye and ear attuned to what is happening around us, and

17. Rom 8:28–29; 2 Cor 3:18.

18. Mulholland, *Shaped by the Word,* 30. Mulholland's book lays out well how Scripture plays a critical role in spiritual formation. On the subject of "spiritual reading" of Scripture (i.e., reading the Bible to be transformed as opposed to just learning about God), see, Peterson, *Eat This Book.*

the other eye and ear watching for and listening to whatever God might want to point out to us or to ask us, rather than the other way around.

Listening to and flowing with the Spirit is a step-by-step process in which we are invited to say "yes" for the next thing God is asking us to do or engage in. Then, and usually only then, after we have said "yes" and have followed through on the Spirit's leading, will we be ready to hear the next timely word or bit of guidance. Our part is to keep listening and be prepared to say "yes."

Listen and cooperate. Listen and cooperate, in one situation after another. Step by step, a long string of saying "yes" to the Holy Spirit becomes a Spirit-led life.

The place to start is with this present moment.

Your next Spirit-led steps

How are you putting yourself in a position where you can listen better for the voice of the Spirit? How ready are you to respond to what you hear? Spirit-led steps are simply your response to however the Holy Spirit is prompting you in the moment.

Practically, the truth that you need to see or hear may come from reading the Bible, a sermon on Sunday, a book or magazine you picked up, or seemingly out of thin air. The Spirit may speak to you by bringing Scripture to mind just when you need to hear a word of encouragement, of faith, of correction, or something else. You may sense God speaking to you as you pour out your concerns to God in prayer and you suddenly experience peace or are given new perspective on your troubling situation. Often, God speaks to me through my wife. God can use your spouse, your children, a parent, a co-worker, a friend, or anyone else to speak just the word(s) you need to hear. The options are endless. The question is, how well are you listening?

Reflect in writing on the questions and suggestions listed below. I highly recommend using a spiritual journal, dedicated to the exclusive purpose of recording your thoughts, questions, inspirations, and prayers that pertain to your relationship with God.[19] No matter what, take some time, create some space, and listen for the voice of God. Ask God to give you the

---

19. For a good resource for both the beginner and the experienced journal writer, see Cepero, *Journaling*.

courage you need to truly listen, and the grace to be able to say "yes" to however the Spirit seems to be leading.

1. Notice what resonated with you in this chapter. How is the Spirit speaking to you or moving within you at this very moment? In the past few days or weeks?

2. How are you responding? How do you want to respond?

3. What Spirit-led step(s) will you commit to taking this week?

2

Be Humble and Open

Humble yourselves, therefore, under God's mighty hand,
that he may lift you up in due time.

1 PETER 5:6

"FRANK" FELT LIKE A fool. As the senior pastor of his church, he felt like he should be the most spiritually mature member of his congregation. He wanted to be the kind of person and leader who could draw from a deep well of wisdom and self-understanding. Instead, he felt shallow. He was embarrassed because he couldn't come up with any ideas for writing an article for his denomination's journal. Whenever he compared himself to other leaders at his level, he felt inadequate and inferior.

At first, Frank tried to cover up how discouraged he really felt. In entering spiritual life coaching, he simply wrote, "I am at a point in my call and spiritual life where I need focus and direction. I believe I need help in going deeper to discover how and where God has called me and desires to use me in mission." All true, and all good. But to actually make real progress toward these goals, Frank also had to look inward as well as look forward. He had to face how he truly felt about himself. He needed to put aside whatever bravado he might be tempted to exhibit to impress me or shield himself from pain. He had to admit that when it came down to it, he simply didn't feel—as he eventually articulated himself—good enough, smart enough, or holy enough to serve in the position he held.

These were very hard things to admit to himself, let alone to anyone else. Yet, doing so made all the difference in Frank's ability to hear the voice of God and receive the help that he needed. Such humility and openness gave him ears to hear what he never could have heard otherwise. Had he put on a front or let his pride keep him in denial of his pain, we would still be talking about his goals but he would never find the heart to pursue them.

What it takes to be able to listen to the Spirit

To get in step with the Spirit, we have to first be listening. To be to able hear, we have to first be humble and open. Frank and many others I have known in similar situations come to experience God in amazing, life-changing ways not because they are spiritual giants or accomplished leaders, and certainly not because they have big egos or are good at controlling their environments. No, those whose lives are transformed by God's presence and power are those who experience God in their weakness, need, and vulnerability. They often have reached the end of their own capacities and are facing the truth about their inadequacies. They are lifted up by God precisely because they humble themselves before God (or are humbled by something they experience) and are now truly open to whatever the Spirit might want to reveal to them.

Be humble

For many of us, we don't have to work at being humble. Life does it to us! Yet, at the same time, sometimes it can be hard to face the truth about our own failings or weaknesses. We are too embarrassed or afraid that we can't bear seeing ourselves in such a light.

However, when we resist humility, we create barriers in our relationship with God. Our pride may create an artificial sense of well-being. Holding an inflated view of ourselves may make us feel better in the moment. Grandiose thinking may energize us as we imagine ourselves to be powerful, accomplished, or highly valued by others. These things might be partly true, but exaggerated notions of ourselves can lock us in our fantasies. When we distance ourselves from reality, we block our ability to ask for and receive from God what we need. In other words, whenever we seek to relate to God from our perceived strengths or assumed superiority to others, we may succeed at burying some of our self-doubt, but the result will be disconnection from ourselves, others, and God.

Jesus warned against holding a prideful, arrogant attitude in his parable of the Pharisee and Publican, and taught that it is only the humble who are helped by God.

> To some who were confident of their own righteousness and looked down on everybody else, Jesus told this parable: "Two men went up to the temple to pray, one a Pharisee and the other a tax collector. The Pharisee stood up and prayed about himself: 'God, I thank you that I am not like other men—robbers, evildoers, adulterers—or even like this tax collector. I fast twice a week and give a tenth of all I get.' But the tax collector stood at a distance. He would not even look up to heaven, but beat his breast and said, 'God, have mercy on me, a sinner.' I tell you that this man, rather than the other, went home justified before God. For everyone who exalts himself will be humbled, and he who humbles himself will be exalted." (Luke 18:9–14)

Similarly, James and Peter each independently expressed what Jesus was teaching in his parable when they said "God opposes the proud but gives grace to the humble."[1]

The flip side of feeling one up to others is feeling one down, seeing ourselves as inferior to others, or being preoccupied with our failures and all the ways we don't seem to be as good, as talented, or as successful as someone else. But this too can be a symptom of pride. If we are distressed to be one down from someone else (even if it is only in our imaginations) and to not be living up to our ideal selves, it may very well mean that our pride is distorting our ability to see and accept ourselves as we are. In other words, if we weren't so full of pride, it wouldn't bother us so much that someone else seems to be "better" than us. It wouldn't grieve us so much when we see flaws in our lives, which clearly every human being on the planet also possesses.

Humility neither compels us to keep up appearances falsely nor disparages us in our own eyes because we cannot compete with others as well as we think we should be able to do. Choosing to be humble is simply being honest about who we are and where we are struggling. We acknowledge our limitations and need for help. We admit that sometimes we are not the persons we would like to be or that other people think that we are. We face the unflattering truth about ourselves that we would rather not see and that we sure hope no one else is seeing either.

1. Jas 4:6; 1 Pet 5:5; cf. Prov 3:34.

For example, if we choose the path of humility, we may have to admit that our work sometimes isn't up to par. We may have to concede that we do not always reflect Christ well in our thoughts and behaviors, and in fact do a disservice to the cause of Christ at times. We may have to acknowledge how the mistakes we've made are adversely affecting others, whether we made them knowingly or not. We will stop trying to bluff our way through hard conversations with others to avoid being exposed or taking responsibility. We will accept that we need others in order to accomplish what God has called us to do or to be more effective in whatever we're doing; and we will be willing to ask for the help we need.

Yet, choosing humility is not self-denigration. Humility before God is simply being honest with ourselves. We will acknowledge both our strengths and victories as well as our limitations and failings. We will appropriately give God credit for the good work God has done in our lives, and we will admit our need for the mercy and grace (help) of God in so many other ways. That's where it starts. Where it goes is a richer, deeper relationship with God, stemming from a beautiful combination of humility before God and confidence from God, a boldness built upon the greatness of God's love and magnitude of God's provision for our spiritual needs through Christ. We bend our knees, and God pulls us to our feet. We acknowledge our unworthiness to demand or expect anything from God and find that we can now hear the voice of the Holy Spirit who wants to minister to us and to lead us.

In admitting the truth about how much he was denigrating himself and how distorted his self-image had become, Frank became better able to hear God's voice again. He humbly exposed the darkness and doubt within himself and opened himself to hear whatever God wanted to say to him. As he did so, he suddenly was able to "focus," "find direction," "go deeper," and "discover God's calling" (his current goals for his life). Only now, instead of trying to slog forward out of a sense of shame and obligation, he experienced a "breath of fresh air" from the Holy Spirit.[2] He neither suppressed what he was struggling with nor affirmed his negative self-image as "true." Rather the oppressive negativity he had been experiencing was swept away by a greater truth that came from God's perspective. When Frank began to look at himself as God did, he was better able to "right size" his perceptions

2. I am indebted to Jack Levison for this way of speaking about one's experience of the Holy Spirit. See Levison, *Fresh Air.*

of his limitations and failings. He was suddenly able to receive the words of mercy, grace, love, and affirmation that he needed to move forward again.

Be open

From genuine humility comes openness. Being open to whatever God might want to say to us and open to however God may want change us through our encounters with the Holy Spirit are critical on the spiritual journey. Openness includes being willing to hear what we may not want to hear or see what we don't want to see. If we're truly open, we will ask the Holy Spirit to show us things about ourselves that are getting in the way of our relationship with Christ and show us the way forward.

In coaching, Frank quickly learned that his struggle for greater depth and for hearing God's call in mission was rooted in misperceptions about himself and about how God wanted to meet his needs and lead him. First, Frank needed to accept himself for who he was and believe God had every intention of working through him fruitfully, in spite of Frank's perceptions that he wasn't good enough, smart enough, or holy enough. He needed to be open to see himself differently than he had, namely that he had a great deal of depth already. The key to his growth was not to develop depth as much as it was to learn how to access what was already there. When it came to confidence and affirmation, he needed to reorient his thinking and find a better source of grounding for his life and ministry. Instead of looking to the praise and attention of others to validate himself, he needed to spend more time with God to sustain and nourish him spiritually. And this is exactly where the Holy Spirit led him.

Frank's experience illustrates the importance and value of humility and openness before God. The Holy Spirit had every intention of ministering to him and strengthening him. The Spirit wanted to build his confidence by first reorienting his self-reliance (which was sagging noticeably) to become more God-reliant, and in so doing help him to see all the reasons he could lead with boldness instead of shame and fear. Yet, none of this would have been possible without Frank's willingness to admit where he was struggling and to open himself up to whatever the Spirit might want to say to him and do in him. And the results were the opposites of his fears, and far exceeded his hopes.

The truth sets us free

Jesus taught that all those who sin are slaves to sin, and need to be set free (John 8:34). To experience freedom, we need to be open to whatever truth the Spirit wants to show us and convince us of—the truth about what God wants for our lives, the truth about what's really going on that may be hindering our relationship with God, and the truth about God's plan to save us from ourselves and our sins.[3] And then comes freedom. As Jesus put it, once we see and embrace the truth God reveals to us, "the truth will set [us] free" (John 8:32). In context, the truth Jesus principally had in mind was to see that he was from "above," i.e., sent by the Father, that salvation comes to those who put their faith in him, and that his true disciples "hold to his teaching" (8:23–31).

Sometimes, our biggest need, then, is for the Holy Spirit to break through our denials, resistance, and blindness—whether unintentional or willful. When we resist and or simply can't face the truth about something that's gone awry in our life, the Holy Spirit can help us to face what we need to face, to repent of our sin, and to be delivered from its crippling power.

In Romans 7, Paul teaches that on our own (by our "flesh"), we do not have the ability to do the good we desire or to resist the pull of our desires toward sin. In chapter 8, in light of our helplessness in the face of the power of sin, he goes on to explain that only faith in Christ enables any of us to escape condemnation. However, that is not the end. The salvation God offers through faith in Christ takes on a practical form in the here and now through the Holy Spirit, through whom we have real power to overcome temptation and sin. Our part is to focus our minds on the Spirit and follow the Spirit's leading, as opposed to focusing on the self-centered, self-gratifying mind-set characteristic of our "flesh."[4] As we do so, we will

---

3. Cf. John 16:7–11, where Jesus explains to his disciples that after he has "gone away," the Counselor (probably a reference to the Holy Spirit) will come to "prove the world wrong about sin and righteousness and judgment" (16:8, NRSV). In other words, one of the roles of the Holy Spirit is to reveal spiritual truth to us when we resist it, and convince us of our need for repentance; this is in addition to the Spirit's roles of leading us to Christ and guiding us ethically, vocationally, or in any number of other practical ways.

4. Craig Keener explains that "the 'way of thinking involving the flesh' is a chronic perspective or disposition from mere human, bodily existence as opposed to a life perspective and disposition informed and led by God's presence. Those whose ultimate interests are purely temporal, satisfying their own desires, contrast with those with interest in and divinely provided access to the eternal God" (*The Mind of the Spirit*, 117).

experience more freedom from the power of sin, which leads to "life and peace" (Rom 8:6).

In Galatians 5, Paul talks again about the critical role of the Spirit in the life of believers in Christ. First he spends a good deal of space describing the contrast between the desires of our "flesh" and the leading of the Spirit. He draws the conclusion that only the Spirit can set us free from the tyranny of sin in our lives and can produce love, joy, peace, and many other wonderful qualities and experiences that can only come from God's activity within us. To be set free from the power of sin by drawing on the Spirit and to experience a new quality of life through the Spirit's influence in our lives is what it means to "live by the Spirit" (Gal 5:16–24). Inasmuch as we can and sometimes do experience this kind of life in the Spirit, he concludes, those who live by the Spirit ought to consciously seek to "keep in step with the Spirit" (Gal 5:25). In other words, since we know what it is to experience new life through the Spirit, we should actively draw upon the power of the Spirit to consistently live in freedom (from sin) and to do whatever good the Spirit might prompt us to do.[5]

We can wait until truth comes crashing down on us, such as when life falls apart in some way or when others we love and care about suffer serious consequences of our living in denial. Or, as a much more helpful and less painful alternative, we can proactively seek to know and live by the truth in every aspect of our lives. We can humble and open ourselves to whatever God wants to reveal to us. We can ask God to help us to see whatever truth we need to see, and to find the strength we need to keep in step with however the Spirit is leading.

The living and active Word of God

When we are truly open to God and are actively listening for God's voice, the Holy Spirit will often reveal truth to us and change our hearts and minds through the Word of God. The universe was created by God who "spoke" the world into existence (Gen 1). Over the centuries, God's Spirit has spoken through prophets to reveal the will of God to his people (e.g., see 2 Pet 1:20–21). "God-breathed" Scripture leads believers to salvation and equips them for spiritual maturity and doing good work in the world (e.g., 2 Tim 3:15–17). According to John's portrayal of Christ, God revealed

---

5. See the introduction, above, for a discussion on how keeping in step with the Spirit is intricately connected to, yet is to be distinguished from, living by the Spirit.

himself to humanity when the "Word" (in Greek, *logos*) became "flesh" and lived among other human beings.[6] Through an encounter with Jesus Christ, the Logos, and by putting their faith in him, believers become children of God (John 1:10–14).

In other words, whether it is the creative activity of God, the spoken (and written) words of God, the very person of God, or the personal guidance of the Holy Spirit, the Word of God works powerfully to reveal truth and create something good and beautiful throughout the universe, especially in human lives. Life comes through the Word of God, we know who God is by the Word of God, we know better what God wants for our lives by the Word of God, and we experience spiritual transformation through our encounters with the Word of God. There is no other resource that comes close to the Word of God in its ability to help us know, love, and serve God as followers of Christ.

We can see how early Christians thought about and relied on the Word of God, particularly in the book of Hebrews. Over and over again, both explicitly in the author's teaching and implicitly in how he used Scripture and preached to his readers, he pointed to the Word of God and relied on the Spirit of God to touch and change his readers' lives.

In the very opening verses of the letter, the author presents to the Hebrews the Son of God, by whom he means Jesus Christ, as the latest and greatest way God has spoken to humanity. He does not use John's language to explicitly refer to the Son as the "Word" (*logos*) of God, but instead links him to the Word of God by saying that "in these last days [God] *has spoken* to us by his Son, whom he appointed heir of all things, and through whom he made the universe" (1:2, italics added). The author then spends more than two chapters explaining how God is working through the Son in order to establish God's kingdom and provide salvation for humanity (1:1–3:6).

In chapters 3 and 4, the author to the Hebrews quotes from the Hebrew Scriptures extensively and refers to the ministry of the Holy Spirit as God's voice (words) to lead hearers to repentance, belief, and salvation (3:7–12). He eventually links the past to the present, the Word of God in history and the Spirit of God in the moment, when he suddenly moves from Old Testament prophecy to its fulfillment in his own time in chapter 4. He

6. John 1:1, 14. Paul similarly described Jesus as the very "image of the invisible God" (Col 1:15). Jesus Christ participates in the work of creation and reveals to us the "fullness of God" (Col 1:16–20). Likewise, the writer to the Hebrews describes the Son as "the radiance of God's glory and exact representation of his being, sustaining all things by his powerful word" (Heb 1:3).

explains that what God said to David about a certain day called "today" is now this day, the time inaugurated by the coming of the Son of God when the message spoken by God in history is suddenly God's Word for the present moment. "Today, if you hear [God's] voice, do not harden your hearts," he preaches (4:7). What is he doing? He is affirming the critical role of the Word of God both through the Holy Spirit and in the written Scriptures to change people's lives, a point he then makes explicit in verses 12–13:

> For the word of God is living and active. Sharper than any double-edged sword, it penetrates even to dividing soul and spirit, joints and marrow; it judges the thoughts and attitudes of the heart. Nothing in all creation is hidden from God's sight. Everything is uncovered and laid bare before the eyes of him to whom we must give account. (Heb 4:12–13)

The writer to the Hebrews does not distinguish among the various meanings of the Word of God in these verses, no doubt because he believes that God's powerful Word comes to us in many different ways. When we encounter the Word of God, all pretense, denial, self-deceit, pride, and shameful secrets are suddenly exposed for what they are. The Spirit of God sees right through us and reveals truth about us. There, humbled and vulnerable, the Word of God also heals our wounds and shows us the way forward. In a word, that healing is in Jesus. The way forward is by faith. In a true encounter with the powerful Word of God we may begin in terror, but we end up with true hope. Our response is not one of pride, negotiation, debate, or bargaining. It must be surrender to the truth that the Word reveals about ourselves and our need. Our faith response is our acknowledgement that God in Christ in the only source of real hope available to us. The writer to the Hebrews puts it this way:

> Therefore, since we have a great high priest who has gone through the heavens, Jesus the Son of God, let us hold firmly to the faith we profess. For we do not have a high priest who is unable to sympathize with our weaknesses, but we have one who has been tempted in every way, just as we are—yet was without sin. (Heb 4:14–15)

Once we understand the truth about both our need and the source of our help, we will know what to do—pray like mad! But the prayer we offer is not one of desperation—though at times we may certainly feel desperate for God's help—or hoping against hope for mercy. No, that would be bad theology and contrary to the whole tenor of the New Testament. God's love is so great, and Jesus' sacrificial act in dying for humanity on the cross so complete and effective, that the writer to the Hebrews can insist that we who have faith in Christ may "approach the throne of grace with confidence, so that we may receive mercy and find grace to help us in our time of need" (Heb 4:16).

In context, these few verses in the middle of Hebrews chapter 4 (verses 14–16) tell us so much about what we need to know to help us in our spiritual life. They indicate that the help we need in our day-by-day journey to better know, love, and serve God as followers of Christ is all found in what Christ has done for us and in our personal relationship with God. Our creator and Savior, who sits on a metaphorical throne representing his rightful place as ruler of the universe, awaits our prayers with open arms. God's kingdom is marked by grace for the needy, not reward for the mighty. It's marked by mercy and forgiveness, not judgment and rejection.

The Word of God elevated, preached, and experienced in the book of Hebrews points us to practical answers to our deepest existential questions about who we are and how to go forward when we feel defeated, lost, or stuck. We know who are in God's presence because we can finally see ourselves as God sees us—dearly loved, accepted, forgiven, and valued. We find what we need—mercy and grace—so that every barrier to our relationship with God is removed, and we have access to the power we need to live according to God's will. We may not yet know how to fully draw on this power to overcome our weaknesses and handle our challenges, but in God's presence we will know that we have come to the right place. Here, at the throne of grace, where our confidence comes from what Jesus, our Savior and High Priest (which to Jewish ears would have meant, supreme advocate on our behalf before God) has done on our behalf, there is real hope.

In the case of the Hebrews, the grace they needed from God was to be able to hold firmly to their faith and to persevere in faithfulness. In the face of pressure from Jewish evangelists and teachers, the Hebrew Christians needed help to "hold unswervingly" to their faith in God's new covenant, grounded in Jesus Christ as the object of their faith and source of their hope.[7] They also needed help to press on toward greater spiritual maturity, to not lose heart in serving Christ's purposes among their fellow believers, and to live honorable and moral lives.[8] As is often true for us, the congregation to whom the author to the Hebrews was writing was in danger intel-

---

7. Heb 4:7, 11; 8:6, 13; 10:18–39.
8. Heb 6:1, 9–12; 13:1–19.

lectually, morally, relationally, and spiritually. They needed God's help in order to face these challenges and come out victoriously on the other side.

The author to the Hebrews, then, shows us by example as well as teaching how much believers must depend on the Word of God—in Scripture, directly through the Spirit, by the Son, via preaching—for salvation and to live out the Christian life. [9] Through the Word of God, believers may experience movement from ignorance to deeper understanding, from humility to healing, from hopelessness to confidence, from alienation to fellowship.[10] This Spirit-led process prods us out of our hiding places and shakes us free from our bondage to self-denial, fear, and sin. The Word of God in the hands of the Holy Spirit brings us into a right relationship with God and prepares us to be able to better listen to and cooperate with the Spirit's voice going forward. This process does not apply only to conversion, where we move from disbelief to belief and trust in Christ, but is a recurring pattern that describes what happens within believers over and over again. Whenever we become aware of our need for God or of something God is calling us to in some new way, the Spirit is drawing us to God and helping us to mature. Our part is to be humble and open to the Spirit's promptings (i.e., listen), and to seek God's help to hold on to our faith and persevere in faithfulness (i.e., cooperate).

9. Not infrequently, the Spirit also attempts to lead us to important truth and to transform us through our encounters with "others," especially those whom we perceive to be different from us or those who make us feel uncomfortable for some reason. Along these lines, retired professor of theology and Methodist minister Frances Young discusses what she learned from grappling with a disabled son and other painful life experiences in her book, *Brokenness & Blessing*. She observes, "A biblical spirituality necessitates openness, receptivity, and mutuality," attitudes that lay the groundwork for transforming our understanding of ourselves and our relationship with God. She concludes, "The rediscovery that God is beyond us, yet reaches out to us in Christ to grasp our hands in the midst of the struggle, even to wound us with his arrow of love, might enable us, both individually and as the body of Christ on earth, to live the way of love and true humility in following Jesus" (121–22).

10. See Nouwen et al., *Spiritual Formation*, where he discusses various "movements" that are markers of spiritual growth. Specifically, he speaks of the spiritual life as the continual movement between three polarities, "the poles of loneliness and solitude, hostility and hospitality, illusion and prayer" (18).

Conclusion

Listening to and cooperating with God is at the heart of Spirit-led living. A simple model to grasp, to be sure, but not so simple or easy when it comes to putting it into practice. Why? Because first we have to be listening, and to listen, we have to be in a state of mind that is truly humble, open, and ready to hear what the Spirit wants to say. Learning to get our own selves out of the way, to quiet the competing voices in our heads, to be willing to stop and change course, to be patient to wait for the voice of the Spirit, or to be willing to step out of our comfort zones is all hard work. We may feel uncomfortable or unsure of ourselves when it comes to listening to the Spirit. We may not be sure what is the voice of the Spirit and what is our own voice. We may be afraid to hear what the Spirit wants to say to us. I often am.

But, with God's help, we can learn. We can grow in our ability to recognize the Spirit's voice, and come to listen without so much fear. While the Holy Spirit will indeed convict us of sin and point out uncomfortable truth to us at times, God is just as likely to bind up our wounds and speak a word of comfort or nourishment when we pour out our hearts in prayer. Our job is not to try to control God's response to our prayers, as if we ever could. No, the Spirit's call is to humble ourselves, open our hearts and minds, and stand ready to respond in whatever ways are most appropriate to the situation at hand. Then we will be much better able to hear whatever we most need to hear, and to experience the Spirit's moving and power to enable us to fulfill God's will and serve Christ's good purposes for our lives.

Frank's humility and openness led him to identify the questions that mattered the most to him and gave him the courage to ask them. Contrary to his fears, the Holy Spirit did not respond by confirming his low self-image. Just the opposite happened. The Holy Spirit surprised him with wonderful words of affirmation, love, and support, leading him to a place of peace and joy that he hadn't known in a long time. Then, over time, the Spirit also helped him to see what changes he needed to make, and could make, in order to serve more effectively. Yet, it was never a shaming or discouraging experience, but rather "ah ha" moments of new clarity and energizing insights that propelled him into action and greater effectiveness.

Your next Spirit-led steps

If you were to humble yourself, what would you admit to yourself? What would you say to God? What help would you ask for?

If you were to open your heart and mind a little more, how would that change how you listen to Scripture? To the Holy Spirit? To the prophets in your life? To those who know you well? What do you think you might hear?

Reflect on these questions in writing, or make a date to talk with a trusted friend or spiritual mentor about your thoughts and how you sense the Spirit stirring you. Identify what being more humble and open before God would look and feel like, and then, as soon as you are ready, do it.

3

Be Discerning

Be transformed by the renewing of your mind. Then you will be able to test and approve what God's will is—his good, pleasing and perfect will.

ROMANS 12:2

A FRIEND OF MINE once gathered his family of four around the television one Saturday night. It was a big day. Everyone was excited. The Holy Spirit had whispered in his ear that this would be a good week to buy lottery tickets. Millions of dollars would be such a huge blessing to this family encumbered with debt and college tuition looming. They would be sure to use some of it to advance the kingdom of God, too! Clutching their tickets, they could hardly wait for the drawing to begin.

What a surprise (to them and no one else) when none of their numbers were selected. What went wrong?

We may raise our eyebrows at what seems like an obvious case of wishful thinking, but who hasn't let their hopes run ahead of their reason at one time or another? We get so emotionally involved with what we're doing that we spiritualize our own desires, biases, and preferences. We conclude that God is leading us forward when we are actually leading ourselves astray.

American songwriters and performers Simon and Garfunkel sum up well this common human tendency in their hit song "The Boxer." The lyrics tell the sad story of a young man who left home to seek an undefined and elusive dream in New York City. The melancholic melody draws attention to his loneliness and struggles in facing the harsh realities of real life. The source of his troubles, common to all of us who deceive ourselves at times, is his own selective listening and wishful thinking. We only hear what we want to hear, and we disregard the rest.

Balancing head and heart

Expecting the Holy Spirit to do our thinking for us is foolish at best, and dangerous at worst. As one poster, created by the Episcopal church, that I saw around Philadelphia when I worked there as a prison chaplain in the early 1980s put it, "Christ died to take away your sins, not your mind!"

In the previous chapter, I stressed the importance of being humble and open to the Holy Spirit. Am I now suggesting that you stop trusting the Holy Spirit to lead and guide you, and instead only use your mind? No, not at all. Rather, I'm cautioning against naiveté, false expectations, and self-deception. As Jack Levison rightly points out, the Holy Spirit does not function separately from our minds, but often (and even usually) works through a process of studying Scripture, careful thinking, and even heated debate among others committed to discerning the will of God.[1] Practically, this insight means that, in any discernment process, instead of just going with our feelings and with what we want to be true, we need to prayerfully use our heads, too.

We need to use our minds to assess what is truly going on in our circumstances and to think through the complexities involved in our options. We also need to use our minds to avoid confusing our desires and wishes with the leading of the Holy Spirit. As most of us have certainly learned over the years, there is often a big difference between what one wants to be true and what is actually true.

Pray more, not less, but don't expect answers to come in the form of sentimental feelings and implausible revelations. And don't expect the Holy Spirit's inspiration and guidance to replace your responsibility to think through your course of action. Ask God to guide you through your rational thought process as well as through your feelings and desires. Listen to those who know you well and who can be a bit more objective. Face whatever truth the Spirit wants to reveal to you, and use your head.

Jesus said, "Be wise as serpents, innocent as doves" (Matt 10:16). And, "Suppose one of you wants to build a tower. Will he not first sit down and estimate the cost to see if he has enough money to complete it?" (Luke 14:28).

1. Levison, *Inspired*, 115.

No matter how experienced you may be, how knowledgeable, how prayerful, or how full of love and compassion, there simply is no substitute for paying attention to the real world, facing the truth, and thinking through what you're doing.

Ellie's dilemma

Ellie had a dream. As a highly capable businesswoman and primary breadwinner in her family she had had to focus on earning enough money to pay the mortgage, pay for extracurricular activities for the kids, and put money away for upcoming college tuition. Now in middle age she was weary. She still had a lot of energy to work, but she was tired of just working to pay bills. She wanted to pursue her dream of opening a women's shelter. She had a big heart for women who didn't have the same opportunities she had, and she wanted to do something with her skills and resources for them.

In spiritual life coaching, Ellie prayed and wrestled with balancing her dream with her family responsibilities. As she dreamt, planned, and let herself get more and more excited about pursuing her vision, she also became increasingly clear about her present reality. As much as she was ready emotionally to take the plunge, it wasn't the right time. She eventually decided that she was going to continue with her high-paying job in the secular business world for now, but that she would keep her dream in her heart and prayers. She would trust God to show her when the right time was to pursue her dream.

So what good was a discernment process for Ellie? If, in the end, she didn't feel free to pursue her vision, what did she really gain by thinking and praying through her desires and inner stirrings? Peace. She gained greater peace about what she was doing, and renewed motivation to sacrifice for the sake of her family. At the same time, she is keeping the vision in her heart, convinced that the Spirit is stirring her for a reason and that someday the time will be right to act on it.

Create a discernment process

What is your discernment process when it comes to making important decisions, exploring new options, or addressing pressing problems or challenges in your life? How are you balancing your head and heart? What are the roles of Scripture and the Holy Spirit in your process?

Alongside traditional methods of discernment, such as weighing pros and cons, thinking through the options, gathering input from others, evaluating opportunities against our highest values and priorities, and praying for God's guidance, the most important component of any Spirit-led discernment process is actually listening for the voice of the Spirit and trusting God to guide us along the way.[2] We should not pray simply to ask the Spirit to tell us what to do—though I frequently find the throw-my-hands-in-the-air-and-plea-for-help prayer to be comforting and helpful, especially when I feel over my head or desperate. Rather, a more mature prayer seeks to tap into the Spirit's wisdom, deeper level understanding, and divine perspective to assess our circumstances, the needs of those around us, and the opportunities God may be placing before us. To these ends, we ask the Spirit to speak to us through Scripture, to give us wisdom as we apply reason, to use others to help us see what we need to see, to bring to mind relevant experiences in our life that could be instructive now, and to give us a Christ-centered perspective on whatever we're thinking about. The Spirit can also help us know how to weight the various inputs we are receiving, and can provide creative, timely, or fresh perspective.

For analytical people, a discernment process may look very rational and logical, resulting in our being able to clearly explain the final decision we are making. For those of us who rely more on gut instinct, we need enough input so that our guts can reliably lead us, even if our process is more subconscious. The Spirit can help us to slow down enough to be sure we are seeking out and drawing upon the most helpful resources available to us. For those of us who need to feel moved, compassion, motivated, inspired, or some other strong feeling in order to feel confident about proceeding, the Spirit can take us to a grounded place where we are well-connected to our hearts as we are processing all the inputs from our discernment process. In my own experience and that of countless people I have counseled and coached over the years, the most reliable indicator of the Spirit's leading, regardless of the exact process used to get there, is the experience of great peace. Once we have made a good decision (for us),

---

2. Many good books have been written on the subject of discerning the will of God, both for individuals and for churches. One that does a particularly good job of helping discerners listen to their bodies as well as their minds and hearts is Liebert's *The Way of Discernment*. Liebert identifies several components in seeking discernment, most of which are within ourselves: our memory, intuition, body, imagination, reason, and feelings; and one outside of ourselves in nature.

suddenly all the struggle is gone and the questions are either answered or no longer carry much power anymore.

Spiritual life coaching methodology[3]

For use in my spiritual life coaching practice and when I do group coaching during "The Spirit-Led Leader" workshops, I've developed a broad ten-step methodology to better discern the will of God for our personal lives as well as for our ministries. Spiritual life coaching methodology is a systematic, multi-dimensional way to get greater clarity in one's calling and vision for life, in keeping with the Apostle Paul's teaching that "the renewing of your mind" is one of the keys to personal transformation and discerning the "good, pleasing, and perfect will of God" (Rom 12:2).

The method breaks down the discernment process into specific steps, each of which begins by inviting the Holy Spirit to speak into multiple dimensions of your life to produce renewal wherever it is most needed and to help you get clarity about God's dreams and visions for your life. You will listen carefully for the Spirit's voice through multiple channels, actively seek to clarify the guidance you receive, and create concrete steps to put your response into action. In all, by using this kind of methodology, you will follow a thoughtful, holistic way to discern a course of action that, by the end, you will be able to more confidently call Spirit-led.[4]

Here are the ten steps:

1. Pray for the Holy Spirit to guide you each step along the way as you seek to develop God-honoring and Christ-serving visions for every aspect of your life. (Don't rush past this first step. Perhaps the most important aspect of executing a thoughtful discernment process is the degree to which your mind is clear and your heart is genuinely connected to the Spirit. At this stage, the primary goal of prayer is not to pray for a certain outcome or even for guidance, but to cross the

---

3. ©Timothy C. Geoffrion, 2006, revised 2016.

4. This methodology is not intended to be used in a rigid, linear fashion. Rather, it serves as a collection of important practical components of any Christ-centered, Spirit-led discernment process. As for the time required to do these steps, you can sketch out all your answers in a single afternoon or two. However, to work the process prayerfully and thoughtfully with substantial depth, three to six months would be a reasonable expectation, depending on how many life areas you explore and what kind of outside input you seek as part of the process.

threshold from autonomous, self-oriented thinking to submitting your will to God's in the context of an actual prayer connection with God.)

2. Prayerfully reflect on Scripture and your life's experiences. Ask yourself: "What do I already know of God's vision for the various aspects of my life?" (Many of life's decisions are not going to be answered by reading the Bible, but Scripture is still foundational in any discernment process. The Bible informs our values, gives us a godly perspective, helps us to determine our priorities, and is a vehicle the Spirit uses to speak to us. Thus, even though we cannot always expect to find a direct answer to our question or present-day concern from reading the Bible, using Scripture thoughtfully means taking time to read select passages on pertinent topics and asking God to speak to you through the readings.)

3. Do a self-inventory. Ask yourself, "If I were to truly face reality, how do I feel about my life in all its major dimensions?" "How satisfied am I?" "What's missing in this or that area?" (For example, ask yourself, "How satisfied am I in my relationship with God?" or "How satisfied am I with my work or service?" You can then ask the same question about every aspect of your life that you want to focus on. The goal here is to get in touch with how you truly feel about what's going on in your life in each of its most important dimensions. Discerning the will of God requires being well grounded in reality and knowing the self—you—that you are offering up to God.)

4. Create a vision. Know your heart's desires. Then dream and imagine new possibilities. Think constructively. Create a specific vision for each major life area: your relationship with God, your vocation; and your key relationships. (For example, if you rated your satisfaction with your relationship with God, your spouse, your children, your work or any other important aspect of your life a "6" on a scale of 1 to 10, then what would make that relationship a "10"? Your vision can simply be whatever you would add or change from the present less-than-satisfying experience to make it a highly satisfying one. Again, the goal is knowing what is in your heart, naming your dreams, expressing your desires, and consciously bringing all of yourself into your interaction with God as a precursor to however the Spirit may wish to alter or shape your dreams and visions.)

5. Identify your mission, based on your vision for each area of your life. Your vision is a picture of your future reality that you are dreaming about. Your mission is the set of actions and activities you will prioritize in order to pursue your vision. (The goal is to think through what your role is day to day if you were to order your life by your vision, and to see if the actions required to bring your vision into reality fit with your giftedness, skills, and other abilities. For example, the mission we created for Faith, Hope, and Love Global Ministries was "to teach, inspire, and encourage ministers and leaders, equipping them to serve Christ more effectively," because our vision is "spiritually vitalized, better equipped leaders serving Christ effectively in strategic positions of influence throughout the world." The mission expresses the primary means [here, teaching, inspiring, and encouraging] that we are using to pursue the vision.)

6. Identify your opportunities, and make a concrete plan. First sketch out the broad outline of how you are going to get from A to Z to pursue your vision and capitalize on your opportunities for each major life area. Then, identify manageable "next steps" that you can take in the near future. (The purpose of this step is to think through what it is going to take, specifically, to pursue your vision and calling. It belongs in the discernment process because it helps you to see if God has opened the necessary doors and if you are prepared to take the needed action to move forward. If not, then your dream may not be God's will for you.)

7. Identify anticipated fears, obstacles, and distractions that threaten to undermine your ability to successfully pursue your vision. Then create strategies to "right size" your fears and handle the challenges. (Many people flounder because of the resistance they encounter and the size of the challenges they meet. Thoughtfulness means taking enough time to anticipate what you are going to have to deal with, as best you can, and decide if you are prepared—or what it will take to get prepared—to start moving forward.)

8. Ask yourself, "What help do I need to effectively pursue my vision?" Get input from others; create accountability structures; get support; ask God to open doors and provide needed resources; take action! (At this point, you are likely past discerning and really getting ready to start going forward. Thoughtfulness means that you recognize that

you cannot succeed alone or in your own strength, and that you must think through what kind of resources and support you are going to need outside of yourself.)

9. Ask yourself, "What else do I need to do to keep moving forward in pursuit of my vision for my life?" (Here the goal is to push yourself to keep thinking through your ideas, desires, dreams, and visions when you might be tempted to just barge forward half-cocked.)

10. Continue praying each step along the way. Ask God to affirm, refine, and reshape your vision. Pray for God to open and close doors, or otherwise direct you as you take each step of faith in pursuit of your vision and of God's will for your life, as best you understand it. (Prayer is not a means to get something from God—an idea, permission, resources, and the like—and then be dispensed with as long as all is going well. Staying well connected to the Spirit and in close communion with Christ through prayer is for every step along our journeys.)

At the same time . . .

Be prepared to step out on faith

Without taking away one bit from all we've been talking about in this chapter about the importance of using our heads as well as our hearts, and of creating and using a thorough discernment process, there are times when the Spirit's leading will come out of the blue and perhaps make sense to no one—and maybe not even to ourselves.

Sometimes, the Spirit may prompt us to do something unheard of or completely creative, not found in Scripture, not tried in our traditions, and perhaps quite unreasonable to reasonable folks. If the proposed idea doesn't "make sense" by our way of thinking, we need to ask ourselves, are there compelling reasons to step into uncharted territory anyway? Without killing our enthusiasm, what safeguards need to be put into place that will limit the risks but will not undermine the power and inspiration of the creative vision?

A risky venture

When I decided to leave my role as executive director of Family Hope Services (TreeHouse), a Christian-based social service agency that works with troubled teenagers in the Minneapolis suburbs, in order to develop a global teaching ministry, I didn't know if I was following a calling, dream, or fantasy. I was pretty sure that I needed to get back to teaching and more direct ministry, but what was the best way to do so? I didn't want to go backwards to a conventional teaching role just because it seemed a safer route. But, how could I be sure that my being creative and taking a risk was truly going forward and not actually running away from the demands of my current position? Would others judge me courageous or foolish?

These and so many other questions and self-doubts swirled in my head, but I was willing to take all the risks if I could just be sure that the Spirit was guiding me. Yet, such confirmation did not come before I had to make a decision. I knew I had to make a change, and I was willing to strike out on my own. I finally concluded that even if I could not answer all my questions with certainty, I would have to trust that God would guide me as I explored and experimented along the way.

However, at the same time, my move was not a blind leap. I had already made three trips to Bulgaria where I taught pastors and spouses and did some leadership coaching with very positive results. Over the previous decade I had developed numerous workshops, courses, and written resources, including publishing two books. I sought the counsel of others, and conducted, this time with my wife, two more experimental mission trips, one to Myanmar (Burma) and the other to the Democratic Republic of the Congo. Finally, the enthusiastic response we received from each ministry venture, combined with affirmation and support from our home church, prompted us to take the next major step.

In 2008, my wife and I created Faith, Hope, and Love Global Ministries as a not-for-profit ministry vehicle, and we ventured forth. Ever since, there have been many ups and downs and surprises, some wonderful, some painful. Yet, over and over again, the step of faith I took to leave my secure job to venture out into the unknown has been affirmed. I have now taught and ministered in eight different countries, often in countries where there is great suffering and need, such as Rwanda, the Congo, Ukraine, Vietnam, Cambodia, and Myanmar. So, on I go, more and more sure of my calling, but open for changes and reconfigurations of how and where we do our various ministries.

At any given point along the way, I may not be sure if the decision I am making is from the Spirit or not. I'm committed to listening and co-operating, in conjunction with the board of directors, as best we can. Yet I regularly have to make decisions based on the information and input I have at the time without always being sure if I am thinking straight or listening well. Sometimes, when I can see clear signs of abundant fruit and blessings through my service, I conclude that God was indeed in the decision—or at least redeemed whatever decision I made (whether it was a faulty process or misinformed in some way). Other times, I discover that I was not sufficiently detached from my own desires and ambitions to hear the Spirit clearly. In retrospect, I can see how I pushed forward with my own will and stopped listening. I got sidetracked or wound up serving myself at the expense of my calling, priorities, and commitments.

What we can expect

In seeking to listen to and cooperate with the Spirit, all of us should expect to stumble, get confused, make mistakes, and sometimes be completely fooled. If we're self-aware and honest enough, we may never have complete assurance that what we're thinking or feeling is truly from God, or whether the decision we made came from the Spirit or from some other source. Truly, discerning the will of God can involve a complex process, requiring a lot of thought and prayer, and every situation is unique.

Perhaps you are struggling with confusion, disappointment, frustration, or hurt from some actions you've taken that you thought were prompted by God, but now question. If so, maybe you need to make some adjustments to your discernment processes. Don't overreact, but don't miss the learning opportunity either.

If you feel yourself in the grips of emotion or driven by your desires to the point where you or others are starting to question your judgment, maybe you need to take a step back and take an honest look at what's going on. For the sake of those you care about, for your sake, and for the sake of whatever work you are doing for Christ in the world, beware of just believing what you want to believe.

Nevertheless, at some point you have to make a decision. You have to take some action. You have to take a chance. No matter how thorough your discernment process may be, there will always come a point when you have to step out in faith without sure and certain knowledge of what God wants you to do. This is where you need to have some guts so that you don't just take the safe option or choose a path with a small vision, and miss out on the full and fruitful life God intends for you.

Conclusion

As we have been saying, "listen and cooperate" is a simple paradigm for Spirit-led living that grounds our relationship with God in Christ and the Holy Spirit's activity in our life. We should trust more in God's leading than in our own mental powers, personality, opportunities, and other resources. Yet, listening for the Spirit does not imply passivity or magical thinking, and simple does not mean easy. Cooperating with the Spirit does not mean that there is not a place—a very important place—for using all of the faculties and resources God has given us to discern the best way forward. This means we need to use our heads as well as listen to our hearts. We need to create and use discernment processes for making major decisions. We need to be willing to wait for God's will to emerge through the process, while remaining open to those less common promptings that persist long enough and consistently enough that we conclude that God is indeed calling us to step out in faith in some new way.

In the end, discerning the will of God cannot be done by following a simple formula. It requires a thoughtful and prayerful process of seeking to be a good steward of the opportunities and resources God has given us, and to do so by staying as connected to the Spirit as possible all along the way.

Your next Spirit-led steps

Where do you need to be more discerning in your life? Do you have a discernment process for making important decisions? Are you using it? If you were to take a step back from whatever decision or issue you are struggling with right now, what might be missing in your process of listening for the voice of the Spirit? How would you advise someone else (if he or she were in your position) to better think and pray through the matter, using both his/her head and heart?

Take some time to reflect on these questions. Write in your journal or sit down with a wise, trusted friend to discuss your thoughts. Identify at least three steps you will take next to be more thoughtful and intentional about some important decision or response in front of you. Then take them!

4

Commit to "Yes"

"I am the Lord's servant," Mary answered.
"May it be to me as you have said."

LUKE 1:38

BILL HAD JUST ABOUT everything most Americans want. He was very successful in business as a bond trader. He had a lovely wife and four children he loved deeply. He lived in an upscale home in the country club neighborhood in Edina, one of the nicest suburbs of Minneapolis. However, he had a gnawing feeling that wouldn't go away. Somewhere along the line he felt called to go into ministry, and he didn't know what to do with the feeling.

Could this truly be a calling from God? He had so many questions. For five years he went round and round. Could he really afford to do it? Could he handle night school for seminary at his age? How would his family feel about the huge drop in income and the change in his status? He tried everything he could think of to talk himself out of it and avoid making a decision. But he had no peace.

As he struggled, several people were very helpful at strategic points. On his third meeting with one of the pastors of his church to discuss his same relentless feelings and questions, Pastor Dave finally blurted, "You keep talking about the same things over and over again. Why don't you just do it?!" Bill suddenly realized, he had no good reason not to.

Still dragging his feet, it took the frankness of a young twenty-two-year-old with mature faith to help him over the final hump. Hearing Bill's hashing and rehashing the same set of discontent and questions, Andrew told him bluntly, "Until you just obey this calling, you will always be restless!" Bill knew he was right. Finally, he was ready to cross the threshold.

From that moment of decision on, Bill felt peace as he had not felt before. One door opened after another, and the wind was suddenly at his back. He went to seminary at night. His wife sacrificially carried more than her share of the load at home. He graduated when half his class dropped out over three years. He made it. Now, ten years later, he feels a tremendous amount of joy and fulfillment having become a second-career pastor. What was once almost unimaginable had now become a reality. When he finally stopped resisting and listened to the Spirit, his life took a turn he will always be deeply grateful for.

What "yes" involves

A "yes" to God may take many different forms, depending on the circumstances, but it will always involve letting go of something in order to take hold of whatever God is holding out to us. At times, our "yes" will simply look like obedience. One can easily find more than 200 references in the Bible to the requirement or expectation of obedience. Jesus himself provides perhaps the best known biblical example of submission to God's will and willingness to obey. As you well know, on the eve of his crucifixion in the garden of Gethsemane, he prayed, "Not as I will, but as you will" (Matt 26:39).

Charles Stanley, senior pastor of a mega-church, First Baptist Church of Atlanta, Georgia, insists that "total dependence and complete surrender" are key to Spirit-led living.[1] In his own personal experience, learning to adopt a "neutral" attitude before God, being willing to lay aside all of his desires and plans, and trusting in God's leading and will above anything he could create, has been key to his ability to serve as a Spirit-led leader. In other words, saying "yes" to God has little to do with the words we use in prayer, and has everything to do with what's in our hearts and minds. "From God's perspective," Stanley explains, "the content of our prayers takes second place to the question of whether or not we are willing to obey Him."[2]

Indeed, if the message that comes back from our prayers is a directive, then, obedience is the only appropriate response. "Pick up the phone and

1. Stanley, *The Spirit-Filled Life*, 6.
2. Ibid., 201.

call her to apologize," for example, tells you exactly what you need to do. "Now!" removes all doubt as to the timing.

Yet, responding to God with our "yes" often involves more than obedience. Listening and cooperating is more than the spiritual equivalents of "Mother, May I" and "Follow the Leader," games we played as children. Foursquare church pastor Ben Dixon explains, God speaks to us for many reasons, not "just to be obeyed." For example, God speaks to us to reveal who he is—his qualities, love, and care for us. The Spirit speaks to us to bring us back to the "narrow path." Often, the Spirit speaks to us so that we might know how and what to offer to others to build them up or minister to them in some way.[3]

Dallas Willard agreed that mere obedience is not the primary guideline for faithful followers. Love is. Listening to God is not primarily about receiving marching orders, but we do it for the purpose of cultivating and maintaining an ever-deepening relationship with God, marked by love, "from which appropriate obedience naturally flows."[4]

Followers of Christ, then, do not simply wait for directives to be mechanically obeyed as robots or mindless slaves. A love-based relationship with God welcomes and even requires our interaction and conscious cooperation. In fact, as Willard puts it, "[our taking] responsibility and initiative are the heart of our relationship with God."[5] God guides us in ways that honors and works with our God-given capacity to think and make decisions that reflect our own will and desire to please God. Willard taught that we may think of the dynamic between God and the freedom of human beings this way:

> Ideally, personal guidance brings things to the desired outcome but, at the same time, allows the other person's mind to be guided to its fullest capacity without coercing that person's will. Thus the outcome is the work of both the individual being guided and the one who is guiding. The individual's uniqueness counts before God and must not be overridden. It remains your life since you have been guided only through your own understanding, deliberations and decisions.[6]

3. Dixon, *Hearing God*, 96ff

4. Willard, *Hearing God*, 14.

5. Ibid., 34.

6. Ibid., 68.

We could also say this divine-human cooperation is really about learning how to flow with the Spirit in a way that brings all of ourselves into our relationship with God while letting the truth of Scripture, the inner presence of Christ, and the leading of the Spirit guide us each step along the way. I particularly like how Richard Rohr, Franciscan friar, author, and expert on Christian spirituality, has expressed this dynamic when he said,

> Surrendering to the divine Flow is not about giving up, giving in, capitulating, becoming a puppet, being naïve, being irresponsible, or stopping all planning and thinking. Surrender is about a peaceful inner opening that keeps the conduit of living water flowing. It is a quiet willingness to trust that you really are a beloved son or a beloved daughter [of God].[7]

What "yes" requires

Learning how to work constructively with the Spirit requires taking responsibility for our lives. We will actively engage in a process of listening and discerning, and ultimately committing ourselves to a course of action. As our relationship with God matures, we will see substantial attitudinal and behavioral changes, and we will develop increased capacity for making wise decisions and serving effectively. The more we become accustomed to listening to God in the micro- as well as macro-dimensions of our lives, and learn to respond accordingly, the more others will be able to see God in us and at work in our lives. As they see how the Spirit is shaping and developing us, they will be more easily believe that God truly is good, beautiful, and loving. The end result of this process of growth is that God is glorified and others may be drawn to Christ by seeing him in us.

All this assumes a certain degree of human freedom and capacity to make choices and to cooperate with the Holy Spirit for the sake of Christ and his kingdom. This is exactly what Paul taught. For example, when he wrote to the Galatians about how they were living out their faith, he reminded them to use their freedom to benefit others. He wrote, "You, my brothers [and sisters], were called to be free. But do not use your freedom to indulge the sinful nature; rather, serve one another in love" (Gal 5:13). To the Philippians, he urged them to consider the interests of others when making decisions and conducting their lives (Phil 2:4). Paul assumed that

7. *Richard Rohr's Daily Meditations*, May 26, 2016.

they had the capacity to obey God's will,[8] and he expected that they would exercise their freedom (from the law) both to obey when he had specific instructions for them and to choose courses of action that fit with godly principles and values in the normal course of daily life.

Over time, Paul also wanted believers to develop internally, something that happens when we have to reflect on what's happening, wrestle with options, make choices, learn from mistakes, experience God's Word and love in our lives personally, and otherwise engage in an active process of applying God's will to real life. By doing so over and over again, we will mature in Christ—not simply as submissive children, who do not think for themselves; but also as those who learn how to make good decisions in keeping with God's priorities, to put our values into practice, and to make choices that correspond to whatever the Spirit is impressing upon us. This is how we "grow up" as Christians.

Paul's vision for the maturing process is well expressed in Ephesians chapter 4. There, the message is clear. Jesus Christ has provided for the spiritual and personal growth of his followers through the Holy Spirit, who works through apostles, prophets, evangelists, pastors and teachers, to build up the body of Christ. The implication is that individual believers and the church as a whole need to listen to them (and thus to the Holy Spirit speaking through them) and then participate freely with the developmental process that ensues (by listening, learning, changing, and serving). He puts it this way:

> It was [Christ] who gave some to be apostles, some to be prophets, some to be evangelists, and some to be pastors and teachers, to prepare God's people for works of service, so that the body of Christ may be built up until we all reach unity in the faith and in the knowledge of the Son of God and become mature, attaining to the whole measure of the fullness of Christ. Then we will no longer be infants, tossed back and forth by the waves, and blown here and there by every wind of teaching and by the cunning and craftiness of men in their deceitful scheming. Instead, speaking the truth in love, we will in all things grow up into him who is the Head, that is, Christ. From him the whole body, joined and held together by every supporting ligament, grows and builds itself up in love, as each part does its work. (Eph 4:11-16)

Not surprisingly, then, when Paul prays for others, we find him praying for their personal growth, meaning he asks God to develop qualities of

---

8. E.g., see Rom 15:18; Gal 5:7; Phil 2:12.

God, especially love, within them. For example, for the Ephesians he prayed that they might grow in their knowledge of and experience of Christ's love (Eph 3:16–19). For the Philippians, he prayed that they might grow in their ability to be loving people, especially in situations that require discernment and thoughtfulness. We read in his letter to them:

> And this is my prayer: that your love may abound more and more in knowledge and depth of insight, so that you may be able to discern what is best and may be pure and blameless until the day of Christ, filled with the fruit of righteousness that comes through Jesus Christ—to the glory and praise of God. (Phil 1:9–11)

Thus, saying "yes" to God involves a dynamic process, which often begins with bending our knees in submission to the will of God, and then continues in an ongoing cycle of listening, cooperating, and growing in response to the Spirit's activity in our lives. Committing to "yes" means we will actively engage with the Holy Spirit with every one of our faculties. We will draw on the Spirit for strength and wisdom in the ongoing, daily struggle between our sinful desires and the will of God. We will look to the Spirit for clarity, perspective, understanding, courage, strength, and whatever else we may need in order to love others and serve Christ in our particular relationships and roles. In a mysterious way, impossible to fully understand, we will take personal responsibility to live as God has called us, while simultaneously acknowledging our utter dependence on God in order to actually succeed. For, as Paul explained to the Philippians, we are called both to "work out [our] salvation with fear and trembling" and to acknowledge that "it is God who works in [us] to will and to act according to his good purpose" (Phil 2:12–13).

Again, what we're talking about is cooperating with God, who takes the initiative to reach out to us in love and with grace, and who is at work within us to enable us to believe in and to follow Christ, by responding appropriately and wholeheartedly to however the Spirit is prompting us. Listening and cooperating in this fashion is at the crux of spiritual formation. The Renovaré school of spiritual development expresses this same truth similarly: "Christian spiritual formation is the process in which believers cooperate with God and one another so that their souls are nourished and their characters are transformed into Christlikeness."[9]

---

9. Parham, *A Spiritual Formation Primer*, 6.

Now, this emphasis on taking responsibility for seeking, knowing, and doing the will of God may be a bit uncomfortable for those who have been trained in spiritual traditions that emphasize both complete surrender to God's will and total dependence on God's leading. For example, Jesuit spiritual director and writer in eighteenth century France, Jean-Pierre de Caussade, taught that spiritual maturity means surrendering to the point of becoming completely passive to what he refers to as providence, as we either wait for the Spirit's leading or simply trust that whatever happens is God's will. Those who "belong wholly to God," he taught, do so "through the complete and total assignment of all rights over [themselves]." For such individuals, "there remains one single duty. It is to keep one's gaze fixed on the master one has chosen and to be constantly listening so as to understand and hear and immediately obey his will."[10] In fact, he goes as far as to say:

> you will never know either from whence you come or where you are going, from what purposes of God divine wisdom has taken you and to where it is leading. All that remains for you to do is passively to surrender yourselves, offering no resistance, without thought, aim, guidance, or direction, acting when it is the moment to act, ceasing when it is the moment to cease, losing when it is the moment to lose; and thus, active or passive, eager or indifferent, reading, writing, talking or silent, never knowing what is going to happen next.

For de Caussade, this kind of surrender, openness, and readiness to respond is the pathway to transformation and perfection (sanctification).[11]

Indeed, de Caussade's teaching may be needed even more today than in his own day. Most of us would benefit greatly by slowing down a bit, quieting ourselves more fully, relinquishing our will and agenda more completely, and waiting more patiently on God's leading before pushing ahead with our own ideas and plans. Yet, de Caussade's counsel should not be interpreted as relinquishing our responsibility for our lives, but rather as one example of taking (the right kind of) action in a process of listening to and cooperating with God.

Again, when I speak of taking responsibility for one's life and personal growth, I am not suggesting that we should move out ahead of the Spirit, that it's up to us to do God's will in our own wisdom and strength, or that we can even make ourselves mature. Rather, I'm talking about a spirit of

10. De Caussade, *Sacrament of the Present Moment*, 9.
11. Ibid., 41.

willingness and readiness to do our part as soon as we know what that is—both as individuals and in groups, both on a moment to moment basis and when pursuing long-term visions and goals. And when our starting point is a desire to live by biblical guidelines and general truth (e.g., love one another, look to the interests of others and not just your own, make good use of your talents, live a life worthy of the Lord, etc.), as opposed to receiving a special revelation or directive from the Spirit, taking responsibility may look different. At such times (which is most of life in my experience), taking responsibility includes proactively creating solutions and taking action, trusting the Spirit to guide us along the way as well as on the front end. Taking responsibility is not instead of waiting on the Spirit and trusting in God, but it is not entirely passive either. Pursuing God actively and seeking to obey God's will requires working in a thoughtful manner that will often include listening to God alone and with other people, developing systems, planning, and consciously working toward greater growth and maturity for ourselves and for those in our care. As we mature, we will not listen for the voice of the Spirit less, but will increasingly be able to draw on the wisdom and skills we have developed by listening to and cooperating with the Spirit over time in a wide variety of contexts.

What "yes" feels like

We have been speaking about the multi-faceted dynamic of saying "yes" to God to indicate that a good relationship with God goes beyond mere obedience to include engaging with and responding to the Spirit with all of our human faculties, as free and responsible adults. Yet there is also another important, practical reason for doing so. We need to get down to what it *feels* like to wrestle with listening to the Spirit and to finally say "yes" so that we can better recognize within ourselves when God is leading and calling for a response from us.

First, we will grow accustomed to hearing helpful thoughts and sensing the need to take this input seriously. We may be conscious of having the freedom to make choices, and the option of saying "yes" or "no" to the Spirit. Sometimes we will feel inner turmoil or tension mounting. Other times, we may feel that the lights have suddenly come on or that we are able to see something we couldn't see before. Other times, the inner change will be a shift in our hearts, toward ourselves or toward someone else. At some point, when we finally grasp the significance of the Spirit's prompting, or we simply accept it as divine guidance, our "yes" will feel like dropping our resistance or simply accepting that we have just been shown the way forward. In non-theological language, saying "yes" to God at such times may simply feel like letting go and "going with the flow" of the Spirit.[12]

When the Spirit was calling Bill to leave a lucrative career in business to become a pastor, he experienced a wide range of feelings. He felt strangely dissatisfied with his life. He no longer took the same pleasure from his work. He was intrigued by the idea of going into ministry and felt attracted to helping other people in a professional context, but was perplexed and insecure. He felt motivation to go forward and resistance at the same time. It was only over time that he was able to name his desires, ask all his questions, admit the extent of his restlessness, and acknowledge that he did in fact know what the Spirit was saying to him. And it was only when he said "yes" to the Spirit and put his "yes" into motion that he was able to feel the kind of peace that convinced him once and for all that he was being Spirit-led and was on track with God's will for his life.

What "yes" might look like day to day

Not all Spirit-led moments are as dramatic and life-changing as Bill's, or as important as finding one's vocation. Spirit-led living is for the micro- as well as the macro-decisions of life, and relates to how we respond in the moment to a situation at hand as well as to a major issue. The need to say "yes" to the Spirit can come up in a hundred little ways in daily life—and should.

Jean-Pierre de Caussade's portrayal of every moment as sacred expressed well this important truth. Each moment of life is to be lived in holy openness to God, in which we await God's leading and want nothing else

---

12. Pastor Rebecca Button Prichard, writing from an explicitly Christian feminist perspective, explores the "felt" dimension of the Spirit's working in the lives of believers in much greater depth than what I've briefly presented here. She focuses on the many sensual images of the Spirit found in Scripture and in other literary sources, sometimes drawing unorthodox conclusions, but all with the goal of addressing an important "missing piece" in most portrayals of the Holy Spirit. Namely, she wants to better ground Christian spirituality in the five senses, and in real-life struggle, pain, and suffering, which are all experienced in the body. In the end, she argues, "life in the Spirit is always about comfort and affliction, encouragement and exhortation, warmth and cleansing, freedom, and discipline" (*Sensing the Spirit*, 8). Those who say "yes" to God do so, she would say, because "the Spirit of God satisfies our hunger and sanctifies our tastes, subverting our desire to resist and our longing to universalize our particularities" (ibid., 75).

but for God's will to be done. In commending the forebears of the Christian faith, he said, "All they knew was that each moment brought its appointed task, faithfully to be accomplished. This was enough for the spiritually minded of those days. All their attention was focused on the present, minute by minute . . . . Constantly prompted by divine impulsion, they found themselves imperceptibly turned towards the next task that God had ready for them at each hour of the day."[13]

Jesus' parable of the Good Samaritan is one of the best biblical examples of what it means to be open and responsive to something God might prompt you to do in the moment without advance notice. Jesus uses the now well-known story to illustrate how a despised member of a mixed race, a Samaritan, wound up being exemplary for the sake of all those who want to love God and their neighbor in concrete ways. By stopping and helping the man beaten and robbed by thieves, the Samaritan loved his "neighbor" far better than the esteemed "pure-blood," Jewish religious leaders, who walked on by the suffering man and left him there in his misery (Luke 10:29–37).

The story illustrates what it means to be open to doing the right thing for a fellow human being in need and to being open to how God may call upon us at a moment's notice. The Samaritan's motivation for stopping was simply "pity" on the unfortunate man lying on the ground (Luke 10:33). Listening in this context meant being open to see the reality of the suffering of others and being moved by someone else's plight. His "yes" response was simply to do the right thing—the loving thing, even at personal sacrifice.

From my observation, responding from compassion or empathy for the suffering of others is part of what it means to be human—at least when we are at our best, for it is equally human to not respond in the face of the needs of others because of our selfishness, anger, or some other personal limitation or agenda. What makes caring for others Spirit-led is when the Spirit helps us to see what we might otherwise ignore, to feel what we might close ourselves off to, and to say "yes" to love, even when it is inconvenient, costly, or risky.

For those who know Scripture well, the Spirit often brings to mind Bible verses or biblical concepts in a timely and helpful way. If we're responsive, the recalled verse can put us in a better mind-set to respond to the situation at hand or to make a loving choice that fits with God's will for our lives. For example, we may hear a quiet voice reminding us to be

13. *The Sacrament of the Present Moment*, 1.

patient and kind when we're about to bite someone's head off (1 Cor 13:4). When we find ourselves hesitant to take a risk when called for, we may hear Yahweh's words to Joshua when his knees were knocking at the prospect of taking over the reins from Moses, "Be strong and courageous" (Josh 1:6).

Sometimes, the Spirit gives us a good kick in the seat when we need it. For example, when we're procrastinating or getting sloppy or apathetic about our work, we may remember Paul's admonition to Timothy to be a "workman who does not need to be ashamed" (2 Tim 2:15). Not infrequently, in the midst of temptation, we may hear something like, "Get out of there!" or something to that effect, possibly even recalling Joseph's example of fleeing temptation when Potiphar's wife tried to seduce him (Gen 39:6–12) or the words of Solomon: "A wise [person] fears the LORD and shuns evil, but a fool is hotheaded and reckless" (Prov 14:16). In the face of relentless temptation, the Spirit may remind us of Peter's admonishment, "abstain from sinful desires, which war against your soul" (1 Pet 2:15).

In my personal experience, the Spirit often provides courage and perspective in intimidating situations. For instance, on my own, when I find myself in situations where someone says something that is contrary to my faith or expresses their own lack of faith, I often turn into a "good listener." But this is not the virtue you might think. What's truly going on is that I feel tightness around my chest. I am listening, but I can also be hiding. My anxiety and fear of conflict have sealed my lips. At such moments, the Spirit reminds me to see the conversation as an opportunity to offer a faith perspective the other person may really need and want to hear. Their sharing their feelings and thoughts is sometimes an invitation for me to share mine—not always, but sometimes. The teaching of Peter rings in my ears, "Always be prepared to give an answer to everyone who asks you to give the reason for the hope that you have" (1 Pet 3:15). I don't try to prove someone else wrong, but the Spirit helps me to "show up" in the conversation, be willing to tell my story and convictions, and contribute something of value to the other person.

On the other hand, one of the most powerful promptings I often get is simply to shut my mouth. I may be tempted to overreact to someone and treat him or her harshly, and the Spirit slows me down. Sometimes, instead of just reacting to what I think the other person is implying, the Spirit may remind me to first listen more carefully. James's wisdom comes to mind in a flash: "Everyone should be quick to listen, slow to speak and slow to become angry" (Jas 1:19).

Scripture is filled with both wonderful treasure and ammunition for the Spirit to use to help us in practical Christian living. I can't stress strongly enough the value of Bible study, daily Bible reading, meditation on Scripture, memorizing Scripture, and posting Bible verses on walls, computer screens, mirrors, and the like. Anything we can do to keep feeding our minds with Scripture gives the Spirit more material to draw on to help us. Even if you don't know Scripture well or for some reason Scripture doesn't stick easily in your mind, bathing your mind with Scripture regularly will go a long way, as will continually exposing yourself to the teaching and writing of others, especially trusted Christian leaders, pastors, and writers.

On many occasions, the Spirit has brought to mind wisdom I have gained from any number of teachers and thinkers outside of Scripture as well. For example, when I catch myself tuning someone out or jumping ahead to what's coming up later, I hear a voice reminding me to "be fully present" to the moment and to the other person—an oft cited maxim in my current cultural context. I suddenly become aware that I've squeezed them out of my heart or mind. At such moments, I usually need to take a breath and create enough space within myself to listen more intently again. I need to let go of my own agenda, or return from wherever I may have let some distraction take me, in order to thoughtfully consider their words and to hear their heart. The Spirit whispers, "Listen for what they mean, not just what they say." "Don't judge. Listen." Or, "Pay attention to what they are saying without words." After all, they may be expressing what's most worth hearing in their body posture, in their tone of voice, or in their eyes.[14]

Listening is hardest for me when I feel threatened by what someone is saying to me. If I feel attacked, criticized, or imposed upon in some way,

---

14. The concept of focusing on the present moment and directing all of our attention to what is happening now, as opposed to focusing on the past or future, has found its way into the popular culture, deriving not only from Christian spirituality but also from certain Eastern philosophies and religions (principally, Buddhism) and practical insights from psychology. Regardless of the original source, there is much to be said for being more "mindful" and for detaching from our judgments, anxieties, and desires so that we can see more clearly, be more peaceful, and not be consumed with our passions, personal agendas, or preoccupation with the past or the future. Jesus himself taught many of the same things. Teaching from an explicitly theistic point of view rooted in ancient Judaism with an eye toward establishing the Kingdom of God, he said, for example, "Do not worry about tomorrow, for tomorrow will worry about itself. Each day has enough trouble of its own" (Matt 6:34). Jesus also taught the people to not judge, to purify their hearts and minds, and to love even their enemies, while personally modeling and teaching compassion, mercy, and forgiveness (see, e.g., Matt 5:7–9, 43–48; 6:14–15, 22–23; 7:1–5; 22:37–39; Luke 6:36).

I instinctively realize that if I take in what they are saying, I may be hurt or have to do something I don't want to do. I will resist hearing whatever is uncomfortable or disruptive to my way of thinking or living. The more I am committed to my attitude, feelings, or behavior, the more I may feel threatened by an opposing view, and the more likely I am to put up a fight. I'm not saying that everything others say is reasonable, fair, or constructive. Not at all. But that's not the issue.

Listening to others is related to listening to God, because God often speaks to us through others. In difficult or painful interchanges, the important matter is to listen for the voice of the Spirit—for whatever is good, right, and true—regardless of whatever packaging, emotions, and noise may accompany the communication. Further, listening for the voice of God in the voice of others helps us to develop more loving relationships and to better show the love of Christ to them. By listening well we show respect and communicate that the thoughts and feelings of the other person matter to us, even if we see things differently at points.

Listening to God in the moment, especially when it requires extra patience and acceptance, is often unglamorous, sometimes stressful, and can even be quite unpleasant. Frequently, no one else but you will know that you bit your tongue or offered a little bit of yourself to someone else out of kindness or compassion. Yet, Spirit-led living is not about what we want or about impressing others. Spirit-led living is about what God wants. And what God wants more than anything else is that we are an instrument of divine love, building up, not tearing down those around us; encouraging, not discouraging those we meet and with whom we interact.

Commit to "yes" while you can

On occasion, Spirit-led living isn't about how we relate to others at all—at least not directly. It's about us, and concerns changes God wants us to make in our lives. Sometimes the message God wants to get through to us comes slowly over years. Sometimes it is jarring and disturbing, and comes quite unexpectedly. It's always an invitation and opportunity.

I was 28 years old. My first son had been born safely the day before. My wife and I were so relieved, since our first child had died in a miscarriage. Now, with a healthy child nestled in my wife's arms, we let ourselves be excited about all that lay ahead for us.

Then I got a call. The voice on the other end of the phone was telling me I had to start radiation treatments immediately. I had ten good years left, the doctor said. After that, the rare skin disease would get nasty. Then I would die.

With one deeply disturbing phone call, the adage "life is short" suddenly became very personal. Not only was I not going to live forever, but, in an instant, my naïveté about my mortality vanished. My time horizon for my life had been shortened by several decades. My son was going to grow up without me. My wife was going to be a young widow. I wanted to throw up.

We've never recovered from that doctor's call in 1986—and don't want to. When the shock wore off, I realized that whatever I most wanted to do in my life, I had better do it, and fast. We stopped dreaming about what we might want to do "one day," and became very serious about pursuing what mattered most to us while we still could. We had today. We didn't know about tomorrow.

My wake-up call eventually led me to a long series of choices that have made all the difference in the world to my life and ministry. I sought counseling, asked others for help, had others lay hands on me and pray for me, and did whatever I could to seek healing and wholeness. Contrary to the expectations of those around me, instead of pulling in to focus only on my physical problems, I opened myself to new possibilities and leading. In prayer, I became convinced that I was being called to a different kind of ministry. Part of my pursuit of healing meant making changes while I still could. I went back to graduate school, took more risks, had a second child, kept seeking discernment and leading from God, and began to relentlessly pursue my dreams and deeper sense of calling.

Today, I am completely free from my disease. My wife and I have raised two sons to adulthood. I earned a PhD in New Testament studies, which has opened doors for me to teach and serve Christ in ways that better fit my heart's desires and have even exceeded my expectations and hopes. Now, decades after that fateful phone call, when flying over the mountains of North Kivu, Congo to teach pastors in the middle of a war zone, or when conducting a Spirit-led leadership workshop in Ukraine, or when teaching a hundred theological students in Myanmar, I realize that God has used suffering in my life to move me to new and surprising places where the desires of my heart and the needs of the world intersect.[15]

15. Many others have said something similar over time. For example, I found on the

Fortunately, we are not all diagnosed with a fatal disease that causes the kind of distress and anguish our family had to go through. But for each of us, our days are still numbered. Each of us has a unique calling, with enough time to fulfill it, if we listen to what the Holy Spirit is saying to us in the midst of our suffering, and take action.

Conclusion

When the Spirit starts prodding and stirring something within us, we won't have rest until we take the prompting seriously. We need to listen long enough to know what the inner turmoil is about, and then cooperate by going with the flow of the leading. Once we are clear about the calling, it will soon be time to commit. Whether the Spirit prompts us with Scripture, brings to mind a biblical story, reminds us of something we once heard or experienced, gives us a new inspiration, or troubles us with an unexpected trial or vision for our lives, Spirit-led living is not just hearing the voice of God. It's also responding appropriately.

Our responsibility is to listen and cooperate. Often we will immediately know what we need to do. At times, though, we may need to think and pray more about the situation at hand. As you well know, sometimes we don't know the best way to show compassion, to speak the truth in love, or act on some other spiritual truth that the Spirit brings to mind. At such times, we need to work together with the Spirit to discover what to do next or where to go for help in determining the best course of action.

As we pursue the matter in prayer, the Spirit may give us the words that need to be spoken, enable us to see something we need to see in a difficult situation, soften our hearts, strengthen our resolve, or equip us in any number of other helpful ways. Other times, the Spirit raises an issue, but expects us to make an effort to think through how we are going to apply the word we are hearing, or to reach out to get counsel from others. The point is, cooperation is not always simply doing something the Spirit directs us to do; it is an ongoing attitude of responsiveness, which requires working with the Spirit step by step until we have determined how we will respond.

---

internet one version from an unknown source: "Where your talents and the needs of the world cross, there lies your vocation." I also found a reference to Frederick Beuchner, who was quoted as saying, "The place God calls you to is the place where your deep gladness and the world's deep hunger meet" (*Wishful Thinking: A Theological ABC*, 95).

Your next Spirit-led steps

What has the Spirit been saying to you recently? What is the Spirit saying now—either on the macro- or micro-level of your life? What word or prompting are you hearing that is calling for your "yes"?

Somewhere within you is a God-given dream for your life, or simply a sense that God wants to take you somewhere you have not yet gone. You may not fully understand it, and it may take years to fulfill it, but you know you are being called. Do you have a recurring prompting or an unfulfilled dream for your life that just won't go away? Do you have a nagging sense that there's something you were made to do, or to create, or to contribute, but you just can't seem to get around to doing? Perhaps, you're even really looking forward to getting to work on it . . . someday.

What would it take for you to turn "someday" into today?

Reflect on the stirrings from this chapter and the questions above. Write down your thoughts in your spiritual journal or discuss them with a trusted friend or spiritual mentor. If you haven't done your homework, do that first. But if you're just waiting for more signs or more certainty, you may never take action. Don't be afraid. Be brave. Take the next step as best as you can discern it, and see what happens.

When Solomon anticipated the daunting task of building the enormous and beautiful first temple, his father, King David, anticipated his fear and gave him these words of encouragement. He said, "Be strong and courageous, and do the work. Do not be afraid or discouraged, for the LORD God, my God, is with you. He will not fail you or forsake you until all the work . . . of the LORD is finished" (1 Chron 28:20).

5

Join the Sacred Love Flow

Dear friends, let us love one another, for love comes from God.
Everyone who loves has been born of God and knows God.
Whoever does not love does not know God, because God is love . . .
No one has ever seen God; but if we love one another,
God lives in us and his love is made complete in us.

1 JOHN 4:7–8, 11–12

ONE DAY I HAD a waking dream of the sacred love flow. I was standing on two rocks, straddling a flowing stream of water. I sensed God's love flowing under me and around me. I could feel the energy. I started to shake. The power was immense.

As I contemplated the prospect of God's love expanding, I was suddenly catapulted into the air by a surging fountain. I almost fell over. The sensation was so powerful. I laughed. I pictured myself as a comical, little figure on my back being held up in the air, helpless to do anything but flail my arms and legs. All I could see was water stretching out in every direction beneath me, and a pale blue sky. I knew God was all around me, but I felt alone and empty. I realized that there was one way to fill the void and find what I was looking for. I had to dive beneath the surface.

I was afraid I would drown, but I intuitively grasped that my only hope was going forward. It was dive, and take my chances; or remain on the surface, still surrounded by God, but unsatisfied.

I chose to trust. I held my breath. I took the plunge. But what I experienced was anything but terror and disaster. As soon as I made the decision,

I found myself underwater, swimming freely. All around me were beautiful fish and coral, lit up somehow by God's light. I could breathe by some miraculous oxygen source. I was completely at peace. I was full of joy.

From my mystical experience, a powerful, new vision for my life emerged. Ever since that day, I've wanted to live in the ocean of God's love, and be filled and overflowing with it. I want others to experience this sacred love in their encounters with me. I want everything I do to be an expression of this love.

The sacred love flow is truly a vision. It's a calling. It's a way of being in the world to which I aspire but often find so frustratingly out of reach and absent from my heart and actions. As I struggle from day to day to make this vision a reality, my life consists of a strange mixture of wonderful experiences of seeing God's love touch me and others mingled with moments of raw selfishness, over-reactions, insensitivity, unkindness, and neglect. Nevertheless, the prospect of living my whole life immersed in the love of God and being a conduit of God's love to others is what I long for more than any other ideal or desire. The vision has become my guiding light. And my daily prayer.

Praying on Purpose

"Lord God,
please help me to live fully,
to love deeply,
and to give freely,
so that everyone I meet today
will know and experience you through me."

Nearly every morning, I pray this prayer to breathe new life into my mind and heart. The words focus my attention outside of myself and draw my attention to the sacred love flow that I want to characterize my life. They reorient me and motivate me. They remind me that my life has meaning in relationship with God, and purpose as I stay focused on reflecting the light and love of Jesus Christ to others.

I developed this prayer during my life coaching training in 2006 as an exercise to put a vision for my life into words. Looking back through the eyes of faith, I believe the Spirit led me to create it as a tool to draw me more easily into the flow of the Spirit from day to day.

Now, your heart's desires may be somewhat different from mine, but I offer this love-focused prayer as a model to draw upon as you create your own prayers. A Spirit-led prayer should come from your heart, express your own vision for your life, and move you forward along a Spirit-led path. It should correspond to scriptural teaching and lead you to rely on the Spirit to fulfill your vision. Let me explain how all this pertains to my daily prayer.

Pray from your heart

Each time I pray my sacred love flow prayer, offering these words has the same effect on me. A smile spreads across my face and my heart expands. Sometimes I even want to raise my arms and say loudly, "Yes! That's what I want for my life!" If I step back and consider all the alternatives to what I might achieve, experience, earn, or have in life, I quickly see that it's God working in me and through me that matters most to me. That's where I have found my greatest joy and feelings of wholeness.

I don't want to depend on my material possessions or on the opinions of others in order to feel good about my life. Those bases for satisfaction or happiness are way too unstable and ultimately unsatisfying. I want a full life as God defines it. I want to learn more and more about how to work with the Holy Spirit so that I can consistently contribute to the lives of others in meaningful ways. I long to experience the magnitude of God's love. I desire to more regularly respond to others in loving ways, from my own family and friends to those I meet along life's journey. I yearn to be free to give more generously to those who are working to make the world a better place and to people who need a helping hand. I'm tired of getting sucked into worrying so much about what others think about me and say about me. I want to stop chasing temporary feel good experiences at the expense of the Spirit-led life of love and purpose.

I cannot know for sure if a prayer that bubbles up from my heart is self-generated or from the Holy Spirit or some collaborative effort between God and me. Does it matter? At the beginning, to express what most authentically comes from my heart is a way of being fully present in the relationship. It's a way of saying, "God, this is my starting place. This is me. This is what's important to me. This is what I am bringing to you." But this should only be the beginning of our prayer.

From our heartfelt or thoughtful beginnings, a Spirit-led prayer is one that God shapes and directs in ways that fit with God's good purposes for us and for others whose lives we touch. We can ask God to mold our prayer so that whatever is not from the Spirit will fall away, and that whatever is from God may grow clearer, larger, and stronger. When we pray with this kind of openness to the Spirit's leading, we can trust that no matter where the prayer began it will become Spirit-led in the ears of God and within us, where God is doing the inner work that we could never do on our own.

Pray biblically

When we look to Scripture to fashion our prayers, it is easy to see that living fully, loving deeply, and giving freely captures so much of what God wants for us. The more we experience these things the more alive we will feel, and the more we can fulfill God's purposes for us.

Jesus said that he came so that we can live fully (John 10:10). When I repeat those words, I think about a life full of loving relationships, worthwhile work, helpful service, meaningful interaction with others, and doing all the good God intends for us to do each day. Living fully also means to experience all of what it means to be human, from laughing with friends to being moved by immense beauty; enjoying the wind in our faces on the lake; being filled with awe in the midst of the forest, the desert, the mountains or the plains; preparing and tasting a sumptuous meal; accomplishing a challenging task; creating something beautiful or useful that corresponds to our own inner creativity; contributing to valued relationships as a good father, mother, son, daughter, friend, neighbor, or co-worker; making love; growing fruits, vegetables, and flowers; or doing absolutely anything in a way that grows out of what it means for us to be human. To ask for a Christ-designed full life is equivalent to praying, "Your will be done," and looking for the Spirit of Christ to lead in every possible way and context.

If we want to please God, Jesus taught that the most important thing we must to do is to love God and others with all of our beings (Matt 22:37–39). When we pray to become more loving, it is an act of worship. When we actively love others, we are closest to God. To love is also the best way to make a difference in the world on a person-to-person basis. Paul taught that the Holy Spirit pours out God's love in our hearts (Rom 5:5) so that we will experience God's love for ourselves and increasingly be able to love others, or better said, so that God will be able to more easily love others through us. Even more, in what is perhaps the best-known passage on love in Western civilization, Paul insisted that not only is love the most important characteristic of a follower of Christ, but that if we don't have it, we are nothing, no matter how much faith or how many spiritual gifts we might possess:

> If I speak in the tongues of men and of angels, but have not love, I am only a resounding gong or a clanging cymbal. If I have the gift of prophecy and can fathom all mysteries and all knowledge, and if I have a faith that can move mountains, but have not love, I am nothing. If I give all I possess to the poor and surrender my body to the flames, but have not love, I gain nothing . . . . And now these three remain: faith, hope and love. But the greatest of these is love. (1 Cor 13:1–3, 13)

Peter then picked up on the love theme in urging his Christian brothers and sisters to not only love, but to "love one another deeply" from their hearts, even to the point of forgiving and helping others. To that end, he also prayed that their relationships would not be undermined by the power of sin, but would be redeemed by the power of love. He writes:

> Now that you have purified yourselves by obeying the truth so that you have sincere love for your brothers, love one another deeply, from the heart . . . because love covers over a multitude of sins. (1 Pet 1:22; 4:8)

When I pray, I ask God to help me to love deeply so that my attention to others won't be superficial or contrived, but genuine, heartfelt, and pure. I also pray to give freely, without hesitation or reluctance, and generously. I want to be more selfless, and less grasping and greedy. Jesus shows us by his example, as well as through his explicit teaching, that self-sacrificial giving is at the core of God's character and his will for Spirit-led followers (Mark 10:43–44). Jesus said that he (the Son of Man) came "not to be served, but to serve, and give his life as a ransom for many" (Mark 10:45), which is why Paul could readily teach the Corinthians that, in light of Jesus' example, Christians should generously give of themselves to others (2 Cor 8:9; 9:6–8).

Depend upon the Holy Spirit

Divine love is something we can try to imitate by following Jesus' example, and, at times, we may feel particularly strong and capable of doing so. However, most of us will have to admit that often we feel quite weak and limited in our efforts to love others despite our best intentions. What's needed in many cases is not to try harder, but to learn how to draw more effectively on the Spirit to be able to love someone else. What we're after in prayer is not strength as much as it is freedom from everything that is holding us back from loving. We're asking for a deeper appreciation of God's grace and generosity to us, along with a willingness and ability to cooperate with the moving of the Spirit within us so that God can more easily love others through us.[1]

Paul taught, "We have this treasure in jars of clay to show that this all-surpassing power is from God and not from us" (2 Cor 4:7). It's the Holy Spirit who makes Jesus shine out through our lives. It's the Spirit who turns our often feeble efforts into something beautiful and life-changing for others. While the the sinful nature produces many different kinds of evil, the Holy Spirit produces life-giving qualities within us and actively loves others through us. If we want to know if we're Spirit-led, then, a good place to start is by looking for evidence of Spirit fruit: "love, joy, peace, patience, kindness, goodness, faithfulness, gentleness, and self-control."[2]

At this point, some readers may be wondering, how can we tell what comes from the Holy Spirit and what comes from our own best efforts? And, when God helps us to love others and do good, is God coming from outside of us or from within us—and if from within us, how are God and humans differentiated from each other? These are really good questions, which have been posed and answered variously among philosophers, theologians, and spiritual guides over the centuries.[3] However, for our purposes

---

1. For more insight into prayer as connecting to the source of love and not just praying for God to do something for us, see May, *The Awakened Heart*. May provided an excellent guide to help readers look to God for the love they need, and offered many practical suggestions for applying Brother Lawrence's spiritual practices in daily life. See, too, Lawrence, *The Practice of the Presence of God*; and Foster, *Prayer*.

2. Gal 5:22–23. As we discussed in a previous chapter, Paul goes to great lengths in several of his letters to contrast life in the Spirit and life in the "flesh" (our sinful nature). Those who reject God and focus on the desires of their sinful nature produce many kinds of evil (e.g., see Rom 1:28–32; 8:5.; Gal 5:16–21. Cf. Eph 4:25–32.) In contrast, those who set their minds on the leading of the Holy Spirit exhibit the fruit of the Spirit listed here to various degrees, and experience "life and peace" (Rom 8:6).

3. In technical language, pantheists (everything is God), panentheists (God is in everything, but may still be differentiated from creation), and classical theists (God is distinct from creation) will always argue about the exact nature of God's relationship to God's creation. Science, Scripture, and human experience all begin with different assumptions and provide different inputs that perpetuate the discussion on an intellectual level without providing any definitive way to resolve the question, other than by

here, we need not attempt to definitively resolve these important questions (if that were even possible). Scripture offers enough guidance on a practical level for us to develop a deeper relationship with God and to learn how to keep in step with the Spirit without having to know (or speculate) on the exact nature of God's presence and working within us—as important as such theological reflection is.[4]

Generally, Scripture ultimately leaves the careful reader with a sense of "both/and" rather than "either/or" as the answer to these questions. Instead of thinking that God is *either* external *or* internal, we should recognize that God is *both* greater than and beyond human creation *and* inseparable from the life of human beings.[5] Instead of thinking that our good work is *either*

---

appealing to dogma. For a good list of philosophical terms used in discussing the nature of God, see http://plato.stanford.edu/entries/panentheism/.

4. In focusing on the practical teaching of the Bible, which sometimes leaves us with unresolvable theological paradoxes, we still have a storehouse full of affirmations about the character of God, values, ethics, and guidance for developing our relationship with God in Christ. There we can find many teachings that we can act upon even if cannot ever adequately understand and express the exact, mysterious interrelationship between God and God's creation.

5. Here, for example, is where theologians talk about the transcendence and immanence of God—God who is distinct from and beyond creation, and God who is present with, among, and even a part of creation to one extent or another. On one extreme, God is seen as principally external to us, a divine being who comes to mortal humans to save them and who teaches them how to love through commandments and in the example of Jesus. Through the Holy Spirit, the transcendent God may become immanent in the lives of believers, transforming and empowering them to do the will of God. On the other side of the theological spectrum, among those who affirm a personal God, some understand God as principally internal and inseparable from human existence. At the extreme, Thomas Merton and Richard Rohr are two notable representatives. Merton said, for example, "we are completely rooted and grounded in [God's] love," even though this is a truth we "are no longer capable of experiencing" (*Love and Living,* 17). Rohr argues that we cannot fully separate God's presence in our lives from our humanness. Just as Jesus was fully God and fully human, so we should view ourselves as sharing in God's divinity—that's our "true self" (as opposed to Merton's "false self" that we mistakenly perceive to be real). Drawing on verses such as 2 Pet 1:3, "[God's] divine power has given us everything we need for life and godliness," Rohr argues that we should actually view ourselves as divine, by which he means that Christ is such a part of us that we must not look at ourselves as merely human. The key to our spiritual growth is to recognize our true selves, reject our "false selves" (the mind-set and behavior we have adopted in our alienation from God), and increasingly live the love that we already are. (For a development of these ideas, see Rohr, *Eager to Love.*) Though the nature of God's presence vis-à-vis human creation is relevant to our understanding of the Holy Spirit and how we view our relationship to God, we cannot go any further into this important subject here. For our purposes, we can note that Christian theologians, wherever they may fall on the

God producing the good in us in us *or* the fruit of human effort, we should acknowledge *both* that every good thing in us comes from God *and* humans are responsible and capable of doing what God has commanded us to do, even if we require help from the Holy Spirit to do it.[6]

When we maintain a distinction between Creator and creation, we remember our human frailty and dependence on the grace of God that saves sinners. We are made in the image of God, but God is not in our image. God is holy and without peer, worthy of our praise and devotion. We aspire to be "one with God" in unity of mind and spirit, and to be sanctified by God, but the New Testament writers never teach that we will ever be absorbed into God or actually become God as some religions teach or imply. In spite of God's presence in all human beings, we are all mired in self-centeredness, self-deception, and willfulness, effectively limiting if not completely undermining our ability to love unconditionally in spite of our best intentions and efforts. We cannot save ourselves. We need Christ and the Spirit (whether the Spirit wells up from within or comes from without) in order to fully experience and absorb God's love for us and, in turn, to offer that kind of unconditional, devoid-of-self-interest (*agape*) love to others, which Paul describes in 1 Corinthians 13.

In Romans, Paul wrote that God demonstrated the magnitude of divine love through Christ's sacrificial death on our behalf, and that "God has poured out his love into our hearts by the Holy Spirit" (Rom 5:5, 8). Thus, God's great love is seen and experienced both in what God does for us (mostly notably in Christ) and as something that God infuses into us. Taking this one step further, John wrote that we are called to demonstrate to others the love we have received and benefited from. Yet, to use John's language, it is only by abiding in the vine (Christ) that we can bear this

---

spectrum, insist that our ability to please God and to become the people God intends for us to become depends on God's active presence and working in our lives. Beyond that, we cannot go. We must stay focused in this book on the practical dynamics involved in interacting with God's Spirit as we experience God in the midst of daily life.

6. On one hand, we cannot breathe without the Spirit of God giving us breath, and our very life is dependent on God's life within in us (e.g., Acts 17:24–28). Even more, for those of us who are "in Christ," we should not ever think of ourselves again as having any life apart from God in Christ (e.g., see Col 3:3–4). We do not have to search the world to find God in it somewhere, but can instead simply look inward, where communion with God may be developed through prayer, contemplation, and meditation. On the other hand, Paul acknowledged in his letter to the Romans that God created human beings with the instinct and ability to do good—and many do, at least on occasion, regardless of religious beliefs or culture (Rom 2:14–15).

kind of fruit (John 15:1–17). In 1 John, we read that the central messages of the Christian faith are that Jesus Christ is the Son of God come in bodily form and that "we should love one another." Again, we are responsible to put this love into action, but our ability to love is constitutive of being in relationship with (i.e., knowing) God and from Christ dwelling within us.[7]

All this means that our ability to live in the sacred love flow depends upon our relationship with God through Christ and the leading of the Holy Spirit—that is, how well we know Christ, let ourselves be transformed in his presence, listen to and cooperate with the Spirit as an everyday occurrence. The Spirit is the only one who can help us to abide in Christ and to exhibit the light and love of Christ. We may be touched by reading Scripture, walking through the woods in nature, seeing a newborn child, benefiting from the kindness of someone else, or experiencing any other wonderful aspect of life, but it is the Holy Spirit that makes the connection for us between the beauty or power of our experience and the author of all life and love. Further, the human spirit, which comes from God, can and often does rise up to offer goodness to others; but it is the Holy Spirit that makes our gestures toward others spiritually transformative experiences for them.

In the end, however we try to understand or express the exact nature of God's presence within a human being, we can affirm that a divine wellspring of love is key to living out God's will—whether intrinsic to human creation or as the fruit of the Spirit of God at work in human beings, whether active and flowing through the lives of believers or lying dormant and hidden for those alienated from God and unaware of God's presence and calling. Practically speaking, for the believer, the notion that Christ is in us (Col 1:27) means that we should look inward for God as well as outward.[8] As the late Robert Mulholland, a well-respected former professor and author, wrote, "Our greatest need then is to return to the deep center of our being, where God's very self is present to us in cruciform love as our true being."[9]

Spirit-led living, then, is not just for times of discernment or big decisions when we need special guidance. It is certainly not to be limited to dreams, visions, or moments of ecstasy. Actively drawing upon the Holy

7. See 1 John 3:11, 23; 4:2–3, 7–12.

8. Amid current discussions among theologians as to whether God is distinct from, inseparable from, or even identical to human creation, nearly all practical theologians value contemplation, meditation, and even inward gazing as ways to better know and connect to God in Christ, who dwells within believers.

9. *The Deeper Journey*, 145.

Spirit is something needed every day, to enable us to hear the truth about our lives and to experience what God wants for us personally and for our relationships. The Spirit is always accessible to us and is key to our ability to fulfill the desires of our hearts, to fruitfully pursue God's vision and purposes for our lives, and to reveal God to us and to others through us. In fact, there is no other way to live in the sacred love flow other than letting the Spirit lead and shine through us.

But don't believe in magic

Certainly, God can work through us at times entirely by God's grace and timing, regardless of our consciousness or even willingness, when it fits with God's good purposes to do so.[10] Yet, normally, Spirit-led living—and entering consistently into the sacred love flow—doesn't just happen. Spirit-led living in practice calls for listening for the voice of God and then working out what we hear, think, wonder about, question, consider, and feel. When it comes to loving others, we can expect the Spirit to prompt us to love on many occasions in many different circumstances. Then, in the absence of any specific inspiration or directive, it is up to us to figure out what is the best way to act on the prompting.

Sometimes, acting in love is pretty straightforward. Sometimes it can get rather complicated and messy. Often, doing the right thing may look quite unspectacular and may be as mundane as mowing the lawn when we said we would, following through on a commitment, changing our schedules to offer a listening ear or to help a neighbor do an errand. Spirit-led loving takes many different forms and requires different levels of conscious effort on our part, depending on the circumstances and need. No matter what, relying on the Spirit to love others through us is not a passive process. Being able to love others as God intends first requires taking the time, regularly, to draw near to God that we may become immersed in God's love as fully as possible. Here is where our spiritual practices, especially prayer, meditation, and contemplation, are so valuable. Then, being able to

---

10. Pharaoh is one of the best-known biblical examples of someone through whom God worked, in spite of his unwillingness to cooperate with Moses. The Scriptures say at times Pharaoh resisted of his own accord, and sometimes it was God who hardened his heart deliberately just to be able to use his recalcitrance to reveal the power of the Lord (See Exod 6:1; 10:1; 11:9; 14:8, etc.).

effectively love others also requires our active cooperation with the Spirit's prompting to love, by reflecting, praying for others, and reaching out.

It's to this working-out process that we now turn.

The Rule of Love

Loving others is not necessarily complicated or strenuous. It can be relaxed while still intentional. Instead of having any particular agenda, we set our intentions on loving the other person in whatever ways present themselves in the normal course of our time together. If we start to feel uptight or anxious, we need to keep breathing and listen carefully to what's being said or expressed in their emotions and body language. When I choose to look at another person through eyes of love, I find it helpful to play over and over again in my head "love him," or "love her." This method helps me to get out of myself and to keep my focus on serving the other person.

At other times, knowing how to best respond to others is not so clear or natural, and not at all easy. Conflict, demands, conflicting priorities, physical or material limitations, emotional exhaustion, and other factors can disrupt our thinking and feelings. We may want to be Spirit-led, but the situation seems complicated or overwhelming. We may want to be loving, but all that comes out of us is tension, anger, fear, or some other alienating or hurtful response. The inner conflict or disappointing efforts to love can be confusing and discouraging.

Here is where the Rule of Love can be very helpful. When loving others doesn't just flow and what to do doesn't seem obvious, the Rule of Love says, *choose to act in ways that are truly in the best interest of the other person while you are waiting for your feelings and personal equilibrium to catch up.* Step back, reflect, listen to your heart, pray, get counsel if need be, and then choose a course of action that best fits with love as Scripture teaches and Jesus modeled. And if you feel stuck, then pray for help.

Loving in practice

It was Wednesday morning, in the middle of the Pastors Leadership Training Conference I was conducting in Rwanda. When I asked God for some word to guide me that day, I was surprised and pleased to hear, "Love the pastors."

How refreshing. How freeing, I thought. I had already done all my preparation work. This was the missing piece!

However, I soon realized that my preoccupation with what I wanted from the week was turning the event into something for me, for my benefit—and my ability to love was diminishing. When we were taking a prayer walk as part of the day's activities, I began to ask God to put love in my heart once again. I realized that praying for help was the only hope I had in order to recover the love that I couldn't seem to access on my own.

Nothing happened at first, but as the day went on, I began to notice that I was thinking and acting differently toward the pastors. At one point, in the middle of a question and answer session, I suddenly realized that I was being more patient, kind, and understanding. I heard a voice in my head say, "Hey, you're loving them!"

I almost laughed aloud. I was delighted by suddenly seeing what God had done. By prompting me to pray earlier in the day and then putting the idea in my head, the Holy Spirit had put into motion an inner shift that allowed me to get back on track with loving them rather than serving myself so much. God had done something in me that I could not do for myself without the Spirit's help.

Another time, after returning from Rwanda, I got a similar message from God calling me to love. This time, I was going to visit some family members for the weekend. Now, I love my family very much, and enjoy being with them. Yet, there are many pitfalls and ways I can go wrong in my attempts to relate well to them.

In the morning, before I caught my flight, I prayed my normal daily prayer, "Lord, please help me to live fully, to love deeply, and to give freely so that [my family members that I'm going to be seeing later today] may know and experience you through me." As soon as the words left my lips, I sensed that God was telling me to relax and stop worrying. The most important thing for me to remember as I went into this family time was to not try to do anything heroic or special, but instead to "simply love them."

I didn't love them perfectly over the course of the weekend. At times, I pulled back into myself and just didn't feel up to reaching out. At times tensions mounted, and even tempers flared. Yet the more I remembered to love them from my heart and in my actions, the smoother everything went. I wasn't afraid to disagree or offer alternative points of view, but I reined in my reactions and kept trying to choose what I thought was good for everyone, not just for me.

The voice in my head kept reminding me: "Love them. Love them."

In neither the Rwandan experience nor in my visit to my family did I ever make a point of telling the group that I was "simply trying to love them." I don't think that would have gone over very well. Typically, my determination to love others is just between God and me. I don't expect that others will ever realize that I have been trying to love them or that they will necessarily make the connection between my prayer, God's love, my love, and what they experience by being with me.

However, sometimes someone notices. For example, at the end of the Rwandan conference, the pastors' spokesperson stood up to offer the customary words of appreciation. Instead of just commenting on the course material, he turned to look directly at me and said, "Because you have loved us, we have come to love you." I was really surprised . . . until I thought about it.

My family visit ended on a similar note. When I was about to board the plane to return home my brother called and asked me if I would be willing to talk on the phone to my ten-year-old nephew. They had just dropped me off at the airport, but apparently he wanted to say something to me. Between sobs, he choked out one more goodbye. He didn't want me to leave. . .

Funny, in both cases, I don't remember doing much of anything to bring about these kinds of reactions. All I did was try to love them.

Asking the right question

The Rule of Love doesn't always supply the content for how to best love someone, but it will at least help orient our thinking and direct our prayers. Asking and praying with the question, "What action could I take that would best express God's love?" reaches to the core of what Spirit-led living is all about in its purest and simplest form. I keep going back to the Rule of Love, not because I'm so loving or spiritually mature, but because on my own, I'm not. I need help. I need a simple way to get the right perspective, quickly, even if I may need some time to sort through complex or confusing situations.

The more we ask ourselves this question of love, the more we will be able to discern the Spirit's voice amid all the other competing voices in our heads and impulses we may feel. The more we genuinely open ourselves to listen for the Spirit's guidance, the more settled and confident we become on how to proceed. And even when we don't feel so sure, if we still believe that our action truly is an act of love, as best as we determine it, we can rest in knowing that we have had tried to be Spirit-led, because we have tried to love.

Conclusion

Amid the din of conflicting internal voices, our reactivity to others, and our incessant tendency to want to serve ourselves, Jesus' teaching on the priority of loving God and others as ourselves offers a simple but practical guideline. He's saying, put God's purposes and the well-being of others first in your thinking and ways of treating them (Mark 12:30–31).

Likewise, the Apostle Paul taught, "Look not only to your own interests, but also to the interests of others" (Phil 2:4). That's the Rule of Love. We need to think about the impact of our words, attitudes, and actions on those our lives touch, and to choose to put their best interest even ahead of our own. It's not natural, but it is possible.

It may be easy to blame others for our negative feelings or critical attitudes toward them. But Jesus' teaching on loving our neighbor and even our enemy doesn't really support that kind of thinking. In the Sermon on the Mount (Matt 5–7), Jesus affirms moral behavior and spoke out harshly against self-centered and unethical actions, but he simply doesn't give us much room to blame someone else for our not trying to love them. To love others is our calling regardless of how others behave, not our reward for their approved or desired behavior.

Ironically, from Jesus' point of view, loving others is not about them, it's about us. It's about our commitment to being people of love, who continually ask God to love others through us more and more. It's about our willingness to humble ourselves and to let God change our hearts, or at least give us the strength to do the right thing even if we can't always feel the love we would like to feel in our hearts. It's about our disciplining ourselves to immerse ourselves in God's sacred love by praying, contemplating, and doing our various spiritual practices regularly, so that we have a deep well of love to draw from.

No matter what our hopes and fears may be for our lives and relationships, the Holy Spirit can help us to tap into the sacred love flow. The Spirit wants to lead us deeper and deeper into experiences of God's love—both for our sake and for the sake of others. In the end, trusting in God's love for us and in the Spirit's desire to love others through us will lead us closer to God and to the life Christ wants for us. Whether or not others ever connect what we're doing and praying for with what God is doing in their lives, God will use our Spirit-led prayers and participation in the sacred love flow for good. God will often use us to exhibit the love and light of Christ and draw others to God through their experience with us.

We are not responsible for how someone else responds to our attempts to love them. Saying "yes" to God means joining the sacred love flow and learning how to let God's love within us to well-up and emerge naturally from our prayers. Our job is to keep moving toward the source of love and position ourselves to join the sacred love flow whenever and however possible. We must continually pray for the grace to live fully, love deeply, and give freely. We must learn how to pray without ceasing. Often there is not one clear answer, or even a "right answer," on how to respond in loving ways to someone else, but as we become increasingly immersed in prayer and love, the Spirit will take us deeper and deeper into God's love and into the sacred love flow over time.

Richard Rohr put it well when he said:

> As you practice contemplation . . . intentionally say yes to God's presence and leading. Outside your times of contemplation, stay in this posture of willingness and openness. Let the hard, consequential questions of our world's suffering stir your love into action. Discover and say yes to your unique way of participating in God's love and healing, which is already working in every life, in every place, and simply asks for you to join.[11]

Your next Spirit-led steps

How is the Spirit drawing you into the sacred love flow? What could you do to connect better with Christ so that you may experience the love and grace of God in deeper ways? How could you be more proactive to cultivate your relationship with God so that you will have more fresh living water in your inner "well" to draw from?

Craft your own intentional prayer for living in the sacred love flow. Start with your vision for living fully, loving deeply, and giving freely—and start praying more "on purpose."

11. *Richard Rohr's Daily Meditations*, May 21, 2016.

- What prayer is coming from your heart?
- What Scripture do you want to draw on for your prayer?
- How will you specifically ask the Holy Spirit for help?

Then, make a list of names and how you might apply the rule of love to those times and situations when you are struggling to know how to respond out of the sacred love flow. Journal your thoughts. Share your prayer, your vision, and your plans with God in prayer, and with a trusted friend or mentor. Then buckle your seat belt. Loving others sometimes can get even harder. It is to these more difficult circumstances that we will turn in the next chapter.

6

Don't Quit on Love

Therefore, as God's chosen people, holy and dearly loved,
clothe yourselves
with compassion, kindness, humility, gentleness and patience.
Bear with each other and forgive whatever grievances you
may have against one another.
Forgive as the Lord forgave you. And over all these virtues
put on love,
which binds them all together in perfect unity.

COLOSSIANS 3:12–14

LOVING PEOPLE CAN BE really hard sometimes.

There's simply no love formula that "works" in every situation. In spite of our best intentions, sometimes we don't know what to do differently. Or, if we do know, we may feel that it's just too hard or exhausting to keep trying. We may have even been quite close at one time, but the relationship isn't working anymore and every encounter is awkward or painful. Sometimes our best efforts to try to love them actually backfire, and the relationship deteriorates even further. At this point, we may feel like giving up completely.

Then, there are those people that are particularly hard to love. It may be a family member, a friend, a neighbor, someone in our church, or maybe a co-worker. There is something about this person that rubs us the wrong way. Sometimes, there are good reasons for our feelings—a history of betrayal, hurt, or mistreatment—in which case, even the slightest comment or look by "hard-to-love" (for us) individuals can stir up a whole rash of negative feelings and even bring out our worst selves. All we have to do is see them and the old feelings of anger, resentment, bitterness, or animosity seem to spring out of nowhere.

When loving others is so difficult, what can we do?

First steps—a practical process for getting started

In 2006, when my wife, two sons, and I walked five hundred miles across northern Spain on the *camino*, the thirty-seven-day journey was an extraordinary spiritual and physical adventure. The journey provided an unparalleled opportunity for us to spend a great deal of time together as a family. It was a life-changing experience, in which most of the profound changes came through a lot of pain and struggle. This was particularly true in our relationships with each other.

Our close proximity under those conditions made it impossible to avoid facing unresolved tensions in our relationships with each other. Blow ups, sulking, withdrawing, blaming one another, followed by more conversation, trying to listen better, many miles to walk and think, praying, and stumbling along under stressful circumstances made the journey a lot harder than we ever imagined. Yet, facing the truth about what we were experiencing with each other and being willing to look for new answers led to some surprising discoveries.

What emerged in particular were four practical steps that anyone can take to improve a broken or difficult relationship. This approach can't address serious relational issues and may not be helpful in casual relationships, but this simple practice has turned out to be quite helpful ever since in my family and work relationships in many different contexts. They are the first steps anyone can take to find a fresh perspective and develop a better attitude toward a "hard-to-love" person.

1. See—The first step is to open our eyes to see people for who they are, not who we want them to be, or who we've caricatured them to be.

2. Accept—We need to let go of any negative emotion we might be carrying from our dislike/disappointment/resentment/frustration etc. arising from the fact that they are not who we want them to be.

3. Appreciate—From a peaceful place of acceptance of another person, we are in a much better place to look for the other person's qualities

and unique gifts and contributions, and to begin to genuinely appreciate something about them.

4. Delight—From an attitude of appreciation, we can now let ourselves actually delight in this or that aspect of their personalities or their way of being in the world.[1]

In my own marriage, this four-step process has been extremely helpful. My wife and I share many things in common, but our personalities are quite different and clash rather easily. Plus, we both like to be in charge. Learning to "see" her for who she is has included giving up my ideas of what I thought a perfect wife should be and even who I thought I was marrying! One of the most helpful things I have tried to do is to consciously set aside my previous expectations for her and start over. I step back and try to see what is real about her. I keep asking her and myself, "Who is Jill?"—not "Who do I want her to be?" but "Who is she, actually?" *(Step one)*

Seeing her for who she truly is leads then to a decision point: will I accept her as she is? A negative answer perpetuates my unhappiness and the tension between us. A positive answer opens the door to greater peace—not resignation, but simply accepting that this is the person she is without a big, negative emotional charge tied to this or that characteristic of hers that has been bothering me. Then it becomes a whole lot easier to stop reacting when she doesn't meet my expectations in one way or the other, or does something that rubs me the wrong way. With this, I trained myself to say, especially when the old reactions flare up, "Well, that's Jill." That is, "That's who she is. I may not like this aspect of her, but I can live with it." *(Step two)*

At this point, the marriage can take a real turn for the better—and ours did. When I was stuck in disappointment or resentment, thinking about all I might want her to be or to do that she wasn't, I was mired in a self-centered, self-seeking pity party. When I let go of what I could not change and chose to focus my attention on her unique gifts, my attitude changed considerably. I was suddenly free to appreciate her tremendous love for me, all that she does for me and for our family, and the many ways that she creatively contributes to the world and to my life. I can still be pretty demanding in our relationship, but this process helps me to step back far enough from myself to see all of who she is (as opposed to who she isn't)

---

1. We may not be able to get to this point with everyone (I can't), but we never will if we don't work the first three steps.

and to feel real gratitude for the gift she is to me and all that she does offer (as opposed to focusing on what I think is missing). (*Step three*)

Then, delighting in her suddenly becomes possible again. In my case, I began to genuinely enjoy many of the idiosyncratic ways Jill gives of herself to love and help me, our family, and many others day after day. There's nobody else quite like her. In fact, her uniqueness is what attracted me in the first place, and what I value so highly. I am now more sure than ever that I wouldn't want to be married to anyone else. (*Step four*)

If we want to love others better, especially those who are "hard-to-love" (for us), we need to being willing to do the hard work of learning how to see, accept, appreciate, and even delight in them. Taking these first steps, in prayer with the help of the Holy Spirit, can start to free us from the negative feelings that are blocking our ability to see others as God sees them. As we listen to and yield to the Spirit's promptings, we are likely to see positive characteristics in the other person that we have been missing or minimizing. As we let go of our resentment and irritation, we will experience a shift in our attitudes and feelings. Sometimes just getting clarity about who the person is and isn't helps us to relax. As we move away from being so critical and reactive, we will find ourselves interacting with them more constructively. While using this tool is mostly designed to help change our perspective and attitude, it's also a start toward love.

Over time, as we continue to bring our struggles with others to God in prayer, the Spirit will take us further into God's love and into the sacred love flow. We will become less concerned about who the other person is and how they contribute (or don't) to our lives, and more interested in how we can be instruments of God's love to them.

This deeper kind of love is seen best when we genuinely forgive others. Whether our forgiveness is an act of our will or, more deeply, an overflow of our hearts, when we offer to others what they do not deserve, for their sake and not (only) our own, we are in the sacred love flow.

A deeper kind of love: forgiveness

After the genocide in 1994, a young man we met years later in Rwanda, "Jeremiah," wanted to kill as many people as possible. After his parents were killed by workers on their farm, he sought to slake his thirst for revenge by joining the army.

One day the man who killed his father came to him asking for forgiveness. A revolver was holstered at Jeremiah's waist. This was his opportunity. But he couldn't do it. By this time, he had become a Christian and left the army. He was teaching children and working as an evangelist. When his elder brother heard that he passed up the chance to get revenge, he was livid. "Why didn't you kill him?" he screamed. Jill and I asked him the same question. His answer was simple, but sincere: "God has forgiven me for so much, how could I not forgive him?"

What forgiveness really means

When we're struggling with forgiving a hard-to-forgive person, remembering how much we have been forgiven can be very helpful. As another incentive, Jesus taught that God even requires us to forgive others in order to receive forgiveness from God.[2] Even still, sometimes it is not enough to know that we "should" forgive as God has forgiven us. It's the truth, but deep-seated resentments or wrong ideas about what forgiveness means and how it works sometimes keep us from genuinely forgiving. We may say the words "I forgive you," but too often resentment, bitterness, or fear is buried deep in our hearts and we don't know how to be any different. If you are struggling in any of these ways, here are ten truths that have helped me and others to let go of past wounds more easily and to (re-)enter the sacred love flow.

---

2. See Matt 6:12–15. I understand Jesus' expectation that we would forgive others not as a requirement to earn salvation, but rather as a very practical teaching on the nature of receiving and experiencing the grace of God. To embrace the gift of God's acceptance, love, and forgiveness means joining the sacred love flow at its source. To not forgive someone else is so contrary to the love of God that we must forcibly cut ourselves off from the source of love (if that were truly possible, which it is not) in order to keep our hearts hardened against someone else. If we cut ourselves off from a genuine connection to Love (God), how should we expect to receive the forgiveness we need for ourselves? (see, e.g., 1 John 4:16–21). If, on the other hand, we take our pain, suffering, resentments, and bitterness to God in prayer, the power of God's love can both heal us and soften our hearts toward others. Jesus' teaching that we must forgive in order to be forgiven by the Father is another way of saying, "Do not harden your heart against your brother or sister, for, if you do, you will so distance yourself from the flow of God's grace and love that they will cease to be of value to you." It remains true that God forgives undeserving sinners, but Jesus' teaching makes clear that those who truly receive what God freely offers will be changed by their encounter with Love.

1. Forgiving others doesn't mean denying the wrong or enabling further abuse. You're not saying that what happened to you wasn't awful, or that you will enable the offenders to continue their abusive behavior by not calling them to account. Rather, forgiveness means that you no longer want to stay stuck in your anger. You want to stop being fueled by harsh, resentful, or vengeful feelings. Holding on to your anger isn't going to make things right; it's only going to make you sick.

2. Forgiveness means forgoing revenge. You stop hoping something bad will happen to "pay them back" or "to make them suffer" for what they did. Instead, you begin praying that God will work in their hearts and minds for good, remembering that "God's kindness leads to repentance" (Rom 2:4) and that Jesus said, "love your enemies, and do good to those who hate you" (Luke 6:27).

3. When you forgive others, you stop holding the offense against them. You decide that you are not going to demand that they "give" you something (an apology, repayment, suffering, or some other kind of "payment") before you will treat them with *agape* love, as described in 1 Corinthians 13. Instead, you choose to be patient, kind, and unselfish; and you refuse to punish them by treating them rudely or vindictively (or passive-aggressively), because you want to be a person of love, regardless of what they have done or have not done.

4. Forgiveness doesn't mean being foolish. You can forgive without necessarily putting yourself in a position to be hurt by them again. You need to know with whom you are dealing and what to expect from this person, so that you can set boundaries for your own well-being and that of others who may depend on you for safety. You may appropriately limit their power to hurt you by not looking for or expecting kindness, goodness, or fair treatment from those who cannot or don't want to love you in return.

5. Forgiving others will set you free from being a prisoner to the past, if you begin to discipline your thinking. For example:

   • Stop ruminating over what has happened. It's not helping.

   • Stop trying to make sense of senseless behavior. It's not possible.

   • Learn whatever you can from what happened, and then stop going over and over the failed or dysfunctional relational dynamic. Such internal churning will wear you down, and gives you nothing in return.

- Maintain at least a neutral attitude toward the person who refuses to apologize, or is unwilling to seek healing in your relationship. Remember that their resistance to taking responsibility for their actions is their problem, and doesn't have to remain yours as well.

6. Remember, the future lies before you. It is healthy for you to grieve what was lost or taken from you. You also need to accept that you do not have the power to change what has happened in the past. Then you can make a conscious decision to start looking forward.

7. Forgiveness, then, means moving on. For example:

- Use your energy to focus on what brings life and joy.

- Cultivate and enjoy your relationships with those who truly love you, enjoy your company, appreciate you, nourish and sustain you, and treat you well.

- Focus your attention on your calling to serve Christ with your unique set of gifts, abilities, resources, and opportunities regardless of whatever that other person thinks, may have said about you, or has done to you.

8. Sometimes we need God to help us to release the poison trapped in our hearts and minds. Ask the Holy Spirit to release you from your attachment to your hurts and disappointments. Seek freedom and healing so that you will not be so controlled by the actions of others, and so that you can focus your energy on developing truly loving relationships.

9. The next step is to genuinely desire good for their life. For those who offer a heartfelt apology, set them free by accepting their gesture. For those who have no interest in admitting their wrongs or apologizing, you can still pray that God will use kindness toward them to lead them to God and to a change of heart, a process Paul referred to in his letter to the Romans (Rom 2:4). If you simply cannot do this, your recourse is always prayer, asking God to do in you what you cannot do on your own.

10. Finally, forgive out of obedience while you wait for the grace to forgive from your heart. No matter how hard or impossible it may be

to "feel" forgiving toward someone, forgiveness can begin as decision and commitment. You can choose to forgive out of obedience to the Holy Spirit, who typically reminds us over and over again to forgive others as we have been forgiven.

In my work in underdeveloped and developing countries, such as Rwanda, the Congo, and Myanmar, I am continually amazed by the capacity of some people to forgive others. In some of the places where I serve, there are have been horrific abuses, ranging from bullying, torture, sexual exploitation, rape, and discrimination to systematic oppression, persecution, and full-fledged genocide. Yet, I'm seeing that in such contexts forgiveness is not a luxury, but a necessity for victims to be able to move forward in their lives. For Christians it is perhaps the number one way believers can follow the leading of the Spirit to put love into action and to stay in the sacred love flow. Forgiveness is also absolutely necessary to bring healing to traumatized communities and churches.

Forgiveness beyond belief

Her husband and children had been killed during the Rwandan genocide in 1994, along with over 800,000 others. Hacked to death actually. In this case, by her next-door neighbor. The killer was sent to prison, but his wife and children still live in the same place.

Every day for fifteen years, "Sarah" had to walk by their house and be reminded of the horror of that night, of all she lost, and of all that she must continue to suffer because of what happened. On top of it all, the killer's wife resented Sarah for causing her husband to go to jail, and was cold and rude toward her.

Then, one day the unthinkable happened. Sarah decided she couldn't take living under this cloud any longer. She took a friend from her church and knocked on her neighbor's door. When the woman saw Sarah standing there, she screamed. She left the door hanging open, ran into the interior of the house, and locked herself in the bathroom. When her children begged her to come out, all she would say was, "Run away. Run away. Don't you know they've come here to kill us!"

Sarah and her friend sat down inside the living room and waited. Yet, when the woman refused to leave the bathroom, they decided to come back later with a different friend who knew the woman well. When Sarah returned the next day, this time the neighbor nervously let her in.

What happened next is beyond my comprehension.

Sarah fell on her knees and began pleading with the woman. With tears streaming down her face, she begged for forgiveness. Sarah was sorry that she had been so judgmental of her neighbor. Could she forgive Sarah?

At this, the neighbor dissolved into tears. "No, no! I should have been the one to go to you to ask for forgiveness," she cried out. "I'm so sorry. I'm so sorry. Please forgive me!"

A miracle was happening.

I can't imagine what it must have been like for Sarah to live next door all those years to the family of the man who killed her husband and children, let alone comprehend living with the memory of their brutal murder. But going to ask the killer's wife for forgiveness?

What in the world was going on?

Yet, there she was. She did it. And in an instant, years of hatred, guilt, shame, fear and grief were transformed. I don't think for a minute that all of their pain is now gone forever, but real healing took place in a way that I had never experienced or heard of before.

Sarah's authentic expression of longing for healing collapsed a seemingly impenetrable wall of judgment and mutual hatred. And in the face of such humility and vulnerability, the neighbor woman refused to cling to her defensive denial and projection of her guilt and shame. Their heartfelt response to one another made real repentance and reconciliation possible.

Just because we can't imagine how God can help in certain dire circumstances doesn't mean the Holy Spirit cannot exceed our imaginations. We serve an unbelievably compassionate and powerful God, who can do unimaginable works of grace in the lives of those who depend on and follow the Holy Spirit's leading.

Conclusion

Loving "hard-to-love" (for us) individuals is, well, hard. We should not expect it to be easy, and Jesus explicitly said that we should not reserve our love for those who love us back. Jesus' teaching on forgiveness is not an ideal that few can live up to, or reserved for minor cases of offense. The call to forgive one another is at the core of human and societal transformation, because it is at the core of a healed relationship with God. Forgiveness is also the number one key to fixing what is broken in so many marriages, families, friendships, and churches—and what is longed for by many who now regret their transgression and offensive behavior against someone else.

Forgiving others does not demand that we put ourselves in harm's way, or even that we will not hold others accountable. Seeking to expose wrong-doing and working for justice is also biblical. What forgiveness means is that we release the poison in our spirits that is killing us and sometimes erupting in hatred and violence toward others. We seek comfort from the Spirit, leave vindication and ultimate justice to God. We ask for the needed grace to immerse ourselves in the sacred love flow for our own healing, to be better able to go on with our lives, and to be conduits of God's love to others.

The key is to stop focusing on what's wrong with the other person or how they have wronged us. We cannot change someone else, and we can't change the past. Our best course of action, our best hope to stay in (or re-enter) the sacred love flow, is to draw closer to God and to focus on what is within our power to do. No matter how we may feel about the other person, we can still actively cultivate loving attitudes and relational skills. We can still choose loving actions, while simultaneously praying for the grace to love and forgive from our hearts as well.

None of us starts here, and few, if any, of us are ever completely freed from being self-centered and self-serving, but the person who makes a practice of listening to the Spirit and follows wherever the Spirit leads will experience real changes in their lives. Even if the changes are not perma-nent and our ability to love fluctuates wildly from situation to situation, those who listen to the Spirit day after day become more self-aware and more Spirit-aware over time. We become better able to draw upon the Spir-it's help to restrain ourselves from being hurtful, to gain a healthier, more constructive perspective, to apologize and make amends when we've hurt someone, and to love more proactively. There will be moments, and more and more of them, where God's love truly is the driving force in our lives.

Prayer, then, is essential for the person who wants to stay in the sacred love flow in the midst of difficult relationships. We must ask God for the grace to get past the hurts and wounds that have been crippling us. We need to ask for freedom from our own self-centeredness, selfish instincts, and self-serving or self-righteous reactions to others, so that we can love others as God loves us. Jesus showed the way, and we have the Holy Spirit to help us to do what we cannot do on our own.

The more consistently we participate in our spiritual practices and disciplines, providing we do so with the intention of listening to and co-operating with God, the more the Spirit will lead us to the cross. There, where we cannot escape the stark, physical reality of Christ's sacrifice for humanity, the cross transforms us—not because it has magical powers, but because in gazing upon Christ in his most vulnerable moment, the Spirit reminds us of our indebtedness to God's mercy and Christ's sacrificial love, and fills us with gratitude. As we experience and reflect upon the magnitude of God's love, dramatically revealed in the crucified Christ, we will be better able to love others for their sake, regardless of whether they deserve our love, understand it, or reciprocate it. In close communion with Christ, we will finally be able to love others as God has loved us.[3]

Your next Spirit-led steps

Who is one "hard-to-love" person in your life? You may be at a complete loss to know what to do differently or you may feel powerless, but you still would like to learn how to let God's love flow more freely through you to him or her. Here are some practical suggestions, beginning with the four-step process leading to loving hard-to-love people.

1. Make a list of their characteristics as fairly and objectively as you can. Who is he? Who is she? Without judging them, try to "see" them for who they are. You have done this step correctly when your list includes both strengths and weaknesses, neutral attributes as well as characteristics that evoke emotions.

2. Let go of all that you've been wanting them to be, and choose to accept that this is the way they are—and who they are likely going to be unless they choose to change. Take a deep breath and release all your pent up feelings as you exhale. Pray for the grace to get to the place where you can observe this person and simply say, "Well, that's _____ (that person's name)." You know you have successfully completed this step when you can mention their name without an emotional charge, and you can think of them without disdain or distress in your judgment of them.

3. See Eph 5:2; 1 John 4:8–19.

3. Now, identify their strengths as you perceive them. What do they contribute to the world or others? What potential do you see? What of their life do you genuinely value, even if they are not offering their best side to you personally? You know you have truly done this if you can feel some positive energy within you as you describe their attributes or contributions.

4. Lastly, from a place of peaceful acceptance and genuine appreciation, is there anything about this person that you actually like or enjoy? Don't try to force this step, but ask God to give you eyes to see what Christ delights in when he sees this person. Pray for freedom to actually enjoy some aspect of that person, too.

If the issue you're struggling with is forgiveness, take some extra time for prayer and contemplation. First close your eyes and take a couple deep breaths to calm and ground yourself. Ask the Holy Spirit to show you what's getting in the way of your letting go and moving on. Plan on staying in this quiet place in silence for at least five full minutes. When you're ready, imagine Christ hanging on the cross. Gaze upon the image in your mind (or actually look at sacred art, a crucifix, or a cross if you have one accessible to you). Don't try to control your thoughts, but simply let the image touch you . . . and move you. Listen for whatever comes to mind. Be ready to take whatever next steps become clear from your time of prayer and contemplation of Christ.

God has already done so much in your life. You have experienced God's love and mercy. If you were to take a moment to think about it, you would be able to name many ways that your life has changed for the better because of your relationship with the God the Father and with Christ. I'm sure that the Holy Spirit has already taught you quite a bit about love and has used you as an instrument of his love to encourage or help others many times.

You've come so far in love. Don't quit now.

PART II

Keeping in Step with the Spirit

7

Overcome Evil with Good

Do not be overcome by evil, but overcome evil with good.

ROMANS 12:21

AS WE CONTINUE ALONG on our spiritual journey, if we are truly moving with the sacred love flow, saying "yes" to God only gets harder, not easier. It may become easier inasmuch as we become more attuned to the Spirit and more used to yielding and following. The more we relax and let God love others through us, the simpler and more joyous our love will become as well. Yet, it gets harder at times, because the tests get tougher. The calls to serve can take us more and more outside of our comfort zones and require more sacrifices than we ever imagined we would be willing to make. But this should not surprise us. The way of Jesus has always been the way of the cross.

How far do you have to go?

Presumed dead, Sakindi was thrown into a latrine filled with piles of other mutilated bodies. Having just witnessed his parents being hacked to death by Hutu *génocidaires*, he was barely hanging on to his own life. As he lay dying from a machete blow to his head, he drifted in and out of consciousness. Sakindi was just twelve years old.

When night fell, his uncle who had been hiding in the forest nearby fished him out of the mass of bodies. He was still breathing and was starting to regain consciousness. Though the killers soon caught up with and murdered his uncle, Sakindi managed to escape. That was only the beginning of his long journey of suffering. In one fateful day, in the midst of 100 days of genocide when somewhere between 800,000 and 1.1 million people were slaughtered in Rwanda, Sakindi had to suddenly grow up—or perish.

He instantly became responsible for his younger three sisters, who also miraculously escaped being slaughtered. First they went to an orphanage of sorts, but soon it had to close due to lack of funds. A kind man took the four children in, but then he died. Since the deceased man's widow simply was not able to take care of them along with her own children, they had to leave her home. On the street, they went from place to place looking for places to sleep wherever they could.

When Sakindi was able to work, they were finally able to rent a small apartment. However, his limited income sometimes meant they had to go without food for two or three days at a stretch. Sakindi also suffered from headaches, and sometimes his nose suddenly started bleeding without warning. He showed us the scar stretching across the top of his head. Doctors say that the throbbing and bleeding are linked to nerve damage caused by the old machete wound. However, his symptoms worsened whenever he worried about where he was going to find shelter and food for his sisters. For years, the doctor's only advice was for him to stop thinking about his problems!

Some solution.

As I listened to his story, I wasn't sure I could handle what he was telling me. I wasn't sure I could face the extent of his suffering and desperation. Meanwhile, at the time, there were 350,000 other orphans in Rwanda with their own stories. If it were not for the occasional kindness of strangers and others who are able to offer the minimum of assistance, many would die. Instead, most of them barely scrape by. All of them continue to suffer.

I felt overwhelmed, and scared. If I gave my heart to him and his sisters, and gave them some money, what else would he want from me? Would I get trapped in a relationship that would demand more from me than I could give—or wanted to give? I had already shocked myself when some of us helped him to buy a small, three-room house (not three bedrooms, but simply three small rooms under a tin roof that leaked, with no kitchen, toilet, furnishings, or floors). Where would his need for our help end, I wondered? And maybe even more scary to me, what toll would caring for such a high-risk family take on my heart?

After listening to his story and making a plan to provide modest support for his sisters and him, we held hands and prayed together. He in Kinyarwanda, my wife, Jill, in French, and I in Franglais.

When we stood up to leave, Sakindi wrapped his arms around me. As we hugged to say goodbye, he clearly did not want to let go. Jill told me that he closed his eyes and put his head on my shoulder as he hung on for dear life for at least sixty seconds. After I made a few tentative taps on his back, signaling that it was time for the hugging to finish, I caught myself. That's not the message I wanted to send at all. Clearly his desire for connection and love was greater than my desire to give it to him—and that was precisely what I was struggling with internally. We were in the sacred love flow, but I wasn't sure I could handle any more. I had to make a choice—hang in there or get out?

I stopped tapping.

What are you going to do?

When I was at the Genocide War Memorial in Kigali and read about the brutal slayings of so many defenseless people, I was shocked. I was angry. I was scared. And I was brokenhearted. Sometimes when I hear about the atrocities being committed or about abuse and neglect by individuals and governments all over the world, I become so full of rage and hatred that I fantasize about swooping in, rescuing the defenseless, and physically destroying the perpetrators. The fantasy makes me feel better in the moment, but it doesn't actually do one thing to help anyone who is suffering. Furthermore, I know that if I let these feelings slide into the real world, such rage and hatred are only going to fuel the fires of violence.

James rebuked his readers by spelling out for them that some reactions work against God's purposes. He said, "your anger does not produce God's righteousness" (Jas 1:20, NRSV). To try to fight evil with a show of force growing out of our rage and distress over injustice, abuse, and atrocities may be a normal response for some of us, but it's not Jesus' way. Jesus stood up against hypocrisy and injustice, but nonetheless taught us to love our enemies and modeled nonviolent resistance, even though it cost him his life.[1]

---

1. Jesus' turning over the tables in the Temple was the closest he ever came to a violent reaction to what he perceived to be wrongdoing. As far we know he didn't hurt anyone, but he was certainly angry and showed it (Mark 11:15; John 2:14–15).

Paul expressed the same radical call to love in the face of evil this way:

> Do not repay anyone evil for evil. Be careful to do what is right in
> the eyes of everybody. If it is possible, as far as it depends on you,
> live at peace with everyone. Do not take revenge, my friends, but
> leave room for God's wrath, for it is written: "It is mine to avenge;
> I will repay," says the Lord. On the contrary: "If your enemy is
> hungry, feed him; if he is thirsty, give him something to drink. In
> doing this, you will heap burning coals on his head." Do not be
> overcome by evil, but overcome evil with good.[2]

I hope I can get to the point where I can show love even to my enemies. That's usually quite a stretch for me. For now, I'm focusing on not being overcome by the evil in the world, and not contributing to it. My prayer is that God will give me the grace to do all the good the Spirit is calling me to do, and that God will use my service in ways that fit with his good purposes for others as well for myself.

In short, instead of rage or violence, I am choosing a different, more constructive, response: resolve. I am resolved to not turn away from suffering, injustice, exploitation, and cruel acts of abuse and neglect when I see or hear of them. I am resolved to focus my attention, energies, and resources on standing up for those who need advocacy and on doing what I can to help. I am resolved to pay better attention to the suffering I cause in others, and to change my ways where I can and apologize whenever I need to. When we say "yes" to our human impulses, we are either going to run away or strike out in anger. When we say "yes" to the Spirit, we are going to face the problems and needs head on, and do something constructive about them. Spirit-led living is neither weak nor rash in the face of evil, it's smart and determined.

Love compels us to action

Sandra Schneiders, professor emerita in the Jesuit School of Theology at the Graduate Theological Union in Berkely, California and pioneer in the academic study of spirituality, captures well the interplay of belief, relationship to God, and relationship to the rest of humanity. Schneiders defines spirituality as one's "lived experience" of faith.[3] As I discussed in *One Step at*

2. Rom 12:18–21. See, too, Prov 25:21; Matt 5:43–44; Luke 6:27, 35.

3. Schneiders, "Discipline," 200.

a Time, spirituality, then, is not just belief, on one extreme, or a collection of religious experiences, on the other; and it certainly isn't the accumulation of religious activities. Rather, our spiritual life is grounded in God's activity on our behalf, is enlivened by our response of faith, and is marked by our experience of seeking to live out the faith in myriad ways, affecting every dimension of our life.[4]

In other words, as we have been saying through this book, spirituality is about Spirit-led living, and Spirit-led living is preeminently about living out our faith in loving, practical ways in response to the needs of others. On one hand, the Spirit will certainly lead us to nurture our relationship with God in a personal way. We need to worship, and we need spiritual disciplines to strengthen and encourage us as we seek to follow Christ. We need guidance and inspiration from reading our Bibles regularly, fellowshipping with other Christians, singing, worshipping God, and praying.[5] Yet, on the other hand, between Sundays, the real measure of our spirituality is in how we live out our faith in the context of our daily life and in our relationships. It's in how we fulfill our duties and responsibilities, and in how we treat one another. It's in our level of compassion and concern for those who suffer from injustice, abuse, and exploitation in our society and globally. We must resist the temptation to measure our spiritual maturity by how much we've learned intellectually, how many spiritual practices we observe, or even how many spiritual "highs" we may have experienced. Instead, what matters most is how much we let the love of God move us and flow through us to others. And in how far we are willing to go to live in the sacred love flow in the face of such need globally.

Where you might not choose to go

In 2012, after finishing the semester in Myanmar, we spent a week in Cambodia to explore the possibility of bringing *The Spirit-Led Leader* workshop to Cambodian pastors. I had been invited by Pastor Quoc, one of my Vietnamese translators who had participated in the training in Ho

4. *One Step at a Time*, 6.

5. For some excellent resources on developing specific spiritual practices and disciplines, see Foster, *Celebration of Discipline*; Parham, *A Spiritual Formation Primer*; and Willard, *Hearing God*. See, too, my discussion on the importance of creating vision for our relationship with God, cultivating our relationship with God, and practicing spiritual disciplines, in *The Spirit-Led Leader*, chapters 1–3.

Chi Minh City (formerly Saigon). His experience in Vietnam convinced him that teaching on Spirit-led leadership would be greatly appreciated in Cambodia as well.

For a year, I resisted going. I did not want to work with a loose association of pastors in a foreign country. Too many things could go wrong. Too many things might fall through the cracks. Pastor Quoc kept asking, and I kept demurring. The church is relatively young and represents only a tiny percentage of the country (less than 1 percent by some estimates). The nation's Khmer population is predominately Buddhist. Some 90 percent of the Christians in the country prior to the genocide were either killed or fled for their lives during Pol Pot's reign of terror (1975–79). Christians have been allowed to worship openly only since 1990. The churches often work independently, they often suffer from disunity, and most pastors do not have formal theological or practical leadership training.

Yet, when my wife wanted to go to visit Angkor Wat, the Holy Spirit tapped me on the shoulder. I sensed that I needed to be open to going where I did not want to go. An exploratory meeting with the pastors wouldn't do any harm. In fact, the reception from the church leaders was exciting. They told us that there was an urgent need for both spiritual vitality and greater depth of spiritual experience for pastors. They wanted us to return as soon as possible.

However, what really moved me to say "yes" to this pastors' group was not the need alone. There's need everywhere, and we receive invitations weekly to collaborate with various pastors, churches, and missions around the world. What I couldn't get out of my head or spirit is what I experienced at the Killing Fields and Torture Center in Phnom Penh.

In fewer than four years, the Khmer Rouge's attempt to socially engineer their country resulted in what is now regarded as one of the greatest genocides in world history. Influenced by Mao Tse Tung's political ideology and oppressive tactics, Pol Pot and the Khmer Rouge effectively killed approximately two million people, roughly 25 percent of the population before the nightmare ended.

What haunts me the most is the mind-boggling, self-defeating, senseless policies; the manipulation of the child soldiers; and the brutality of the torture and killings. A dark, heavy sense of evil clouded the whole country for those years and still lingers today in the memories of traumatized survivors. Almost forty years later, Cambodians are still fearful of running afoul of corrupt leaders, and many of the chief perpetrators are still to be held accountable. Justice is still a long way away, and healing even further. Forgiveness is inconceivable.

By the time we had finished touring the prison, I couldn't talk. I choked back the tears walking through the courtyard, unable to get the graphic pictures out of my mind. In the cab, I finally broke down and sobbed in the back seat. It was all so senseless, brutal, heartbreaking . . . and frightening.

I had good reasons not to go to Cambodia, but I felt compelled by love to go where I did not want to go. The Holy Spirit touched my heart and helped me to see the great suffering of these people. God put love in my heart to want to help in some way, and then confirmed the calling by opening doors, providing resources, and leading me to the right people to serve as my partners.

Jesus is our guide and example

After Jesus learned of the death of his cousin and close friend, John the Baptist, and his disciples came back from an intense time of mission work, he decided they all needed to get away for awhile. They needed some time to rest in a quiet place. So they got into a boat to head for a solitary place, where they could be alone (Mark 6:31–32).

Yet, we read that before Jesus and his disciples could even get out of the boat, another crowd had caught up to them. On the spot, Jesus postponed their time away. Why? Because of what he saw and what he felt.

> When Jesus landed and saw a large crowd, he had compassion on them, because they were like sheep without a shepherd. So he began teaching them many things. By this time it was late in the day, so his disciples came to him. "This is a remote place," they said, "and it's already very late. Send the people away so they can go to the surrounding countryside and villages and buy themselves something to eat." But he answered, "You give them something to eat." (Mark 6:34–37)

Jesus' life is one story after another of living in the sacred love flow. He came as a servant and responded with compassion to the needs he saw all around him. He defined his own mission in terms of giving hope and help to those who most needed it. In a Nazareth synagogue, he read from Isaiah and explained that he was the fulfillment of the messianic prophecy recorded in chapter 61.

[Jesus] went to Nazareth, where he had been brought up, and on the Sabbath day he went into the synagogue, as was his custom. And he stood up to read. The scroll of the prophet Isaiah was handed to him. Unrolling it, he found the place where it is written:

"The Spirit of the Lord is on me,
because he has anointed me
to preach good news to the poor.
He has sent me to proclaim freedom for the prisoners
and recovery of sight for the blind,
to release the oppressed,
to proclaim the year of the Lord's favor."

Then he rolled up the scroll, gave it back to the attendant and sat down. The eyes of everyone in the synagogue were fastened on him, and he began by saying to them, "Today this scripture is fulfilled in your hearing." (Luke 4:16–21)

In urging the Corinthians to imitate his example, Paul summed up the self-giving, compassionate love of Christ this way: "For you know the grace of our Lord Jesus Christ, that though he was rich, yet for your sakes he became poor, so that you through his poverty might become rich" (2 Cor 8:9).

At heart, Spirit-led living is letting the Spirit of Christ move us in the same way it moved Jesus. We will set aside our own agendas and comforts out of compassion for those who are struggling and suffering around us and throughout the world. Spirit-led living is a life of love where we regularly respond from our hearts to those who are need. Drawing on the resources God gives us and what the Holy Spirit does through us, we do what we can.

Spirit-led living in everyday life is not trying to save the world—something only Jesus can do anyway. Nor is being led by the Spirit only doing what we can do in our own strength. Sometimes, even often, the Spirit may lead us to face problems and needs greater than our abilities to address, but will call us to respond anyway. Keeping in step with the Spirit in such situations means stepping forward in faith, trusting God to work through us in ways that may seem impossible or improbable to us.

Conclusion

Today is the only day we have for sure. In the face of loss of life, destroyed homes, broken relationships, famines, and other crippling disasters, it's easy to feel overwhelmed. It's easy to think that there's no point in trying to help. It's easy to despair. But, a Spirit-led person does not focus on what cannot be fixed or done, but always asks the question, "What is possible?"

The truth is, there is almost always something that we can do, even in the midst of the worst tragedies and most overwhelming circumstances. Even if it is just showing up to hold the hand of someone who is suffering or to sit by their side in the hospital. When the Holy Spirit fills our hearts with love and compassion for those who are suffering, there is almost always some loving response available to us.

And what is within our power to do is all that we are responsible for. Each of us can do something for some situation that we care about. By writing letters or emails, making phone calls, contributing time and money, offering a smile or gentle touch, volunteering, or simply showing up with willingness to help, we can stand in solidarity with those who are suffering. We can link arms with those who are trying to do something to make a better world.

The Apostle Paul taught that God has equipped each believer with an ability to contribute meaningfully in this world. Paul encourages us to believe in this message of hope, and to fulfill our calling by acting on the opportunities we are given. Here are just three examples of Paul's teaching found in three of his letters:

> We have different gifts, according to the grace given us. If a [person's] gift is prophesying, let him use it in proportion to his faith. If it is serving, let him serve; if it is teaching, let him teach; if it is encouraging, let him encourage; if it is contributing to the needs of others, let him give generously; if it is leadership, let him govern diligently; if it is showing mercy, let him do it cheerfully. Love must be sincere. Hate what is evil; cling to what is good . . . . Do not be overcome by evil, but overcome evil with good. (Rom 12:6–9, 21)

> For we are God's workmanship, created in Christ Jesus to do good works, which God prepared in advance for us to do. (Eph 2:10)

> Let us not become weary in doing good, for at the proper time we will reap a harvest if we do not give up. Therefore, as we have opportunity, let us do good to all people, especially to those who belong to the family of believers. (Gal 6:9–10)

If we let the suffering of others just enrage us, depress us, drive us into ourselves, or we simply try to shut out the pain, we are being overcome by evil. If, instead, we ask God for the grace to stay present to the pain and then for wisdom to know what good we can do, we are on our way to overcoming evil with good.

What can anyone do in the face of widespread evil throughout the world?

Whatever we can.

Your next Spirit-led steps

Ed Sladek, a longtime, good friend and now retired pastor, wrote to me after reviewing this chapter in an earlier version. In the process of offering numerous helpful comments, he added, "I've come to see that being a Christian means that when you encounter suffering and injustice you move toward it rather than away. As with firefighters and police, we are called to run towards the fire rather than away."

How are you being moved by the suffering of others? How is the Spirit prompting you to respond to the troubles of the world? You may feel powerless to stop whatever is going on, but what options are available to you to bring some light or love into the darkness?

If you are feeling overwhelmed by the magnitude of evil, suffering, and need in the world, ask the Spirit to help you to focus on where you can make a difference and how you could be a better steward of your gifts, skills, and resources. Ask for the grace to accept that you can only do so much, and for the grace to trust more in what God can do through you than in what you can do in your own strength.

Reflect on these things, and write down your thoughts and feelings in your spiritual journal. Write out a prayer to God that expresses your struggles with evil in some form as well as your request for the help you need to respond constructively. Share it with a trusted friend or mentor. Do something concretely for someone who is particularly suffering, before the week is over.

8

Take Sin and Grace Seriously

Dear friends, I urge you, as aliens and strangers in the world, to abstain from sinful desires, which war against your soul.

1 PETER 2:11

BY NOW, I HOPE you are seeing how much saying "yes" to God is really about joining and remaining in the sacred love flow, even when and especially when it gets tough. Saying "yes" to God means letting go of all those misconceptions, biases, and selfish desires that hold us back, so that we are freer to flow with the Spirit, and to truly love others for their sake. But sometimes what's holding us back is not ignorance or self-centeredness alone. Sometimes it's sin—outright, deliberate, God-defying behavior that undermines our ability to love, and even produces the polar opposite of love. What do we do then?

A pastor's grief

We had just finished a meaningful, yet challenging week of Spirit-Led Leadership training in an underdeveloped country. The pastors and Christian leaders were very engaged. Many were enthusiastic from the beginning. A few resisted the new teaching until suddenly the Holy Spirit opened their hearts and minds. By the end, significant changes had taken place for many of the participants.

Then there was Pastor "Derrick." Nice enough, funny, and capable, he had nevertheless resisted the teaching and my leadership most of the week.

At times he vocally objected to something I said in inappropriate ways. At other times he showed his displeasure by passive-aggressively withdrawing. I couldn't tell what was going on, and nothing I did seemed to make a difference. A few times, I felt so annoyed I wanted to lash out at him. Fortunately, a voice in my head kept reminding me: "Keep your cool. Keep trying to love him. Pray for him."

On the final day, after we had ended the course, Derrick surprised me by asking to talk with me privately. I didn't know what to anticipate, but I certainly wasn't expecting what came out. Apparently, Derrick felt that so much of what I talked about during the week seemed to be directed just to him. "Thank you," he added, "I really needed to be here." What a shock!

What did not surprise me, however, is what came next. He asked to go for a walk. As we made our way onto the pathway that led away from the conference center, he began to open up. Something was really wrong in his life, and all week long he had been struggling with the Holy Spirit. Sometimes he resisted the prompting while other times he reached out for God's help. We found a place to sit. In the privacy of our booth in an empty restaurant, now far away from everyone else, he began to tell me his story of infidelity, betrayal, regret, and discouragement.

As his words flowed out faster, his sobs grew louder. His tears flowed more and more freely. This young pastor's heart was broken. The damage done was of his own doing, and he knew it. An encounter with a prostitute left him shaken and distressed. What he thought would bring him so much satisfaction and delight was now tearing him apart. He loved his wife. He wanted to protect her, but he had failed her miserably and betrayed her trust. He was so filled with guilt and grief over what happened that he was beside himself. What was he going to do now?

Cat Stevens sang a song decades ago, *Longer Boats*, about unwanted changes coming on a group of people. He included a stanza about a sexual liaison between a young woman named Mary and an unnamed minister. Consensual or not, the young woman and the parson crossed a line, and now they had to live with the consequences. The haunting melody bore a heaviness from regretted acts that can't be undone. In just a few lyrics he points to the guilt and despair the minister was feeling, with nowhere to go for relief or help. This was Derrick.

As we sat together, Derrick's distress and grief were almost palpable. On top of his moral failure, he now had lost heart for his ministry. He wasn't sure what to do. His talking to me was a cry for help, a desperate search for forgiveness and hope. He was on the verge of despair.

When life feels hopeless

Derrick's story is not unique. Even the most sincere and dedicated followers of Christ can and do, on occasion, fall into sin. Not everyone's sin is the same, but everyone is vulnerable, and no one perfectly obeys Christ and always lives in sync with the Spirit—as you and I well know from our own personal experience.

All of us also know the experience of harboring resentment, bitterness, hatred, jealousy, envy, or any number of attitudes that are contrary to the Rule of Love. Worse, at times, some of us may even be actively engaged in regular lying, stealing, sexual immorality, or otherwise hurting others or violating the trust and covenant between another individual, our work, our church, or our broader community and us. We may be quite good at minimizing our misdeeds or conveniently turning a blind eye to how others are affected by our actions. Yet, in our honest moments, there is not one of us who does not know that there is a gap, sometimes a significant gap, between our ideals and our behavior, and between our commitment to Christ and the ways that we live out our faith from day to day.

Being defeated by some sin, whether it is one time or on an ongoing basis, does not nullify our calls to live in the sacred love flow. Yet, most sins we commit are the antithesis of love, and being mired in sinful patterns of behavior undermine our best intentions to be loving people. How can we hope to be Spirit-led conduits of God's love to the world, when we feel powerless in the face of our sinful desires and impulses?

A lesson from Simon the Sorcerer

If we take for guidance Peter's counsel to Simon the Sorcerer, a recent convert to the Christian faith, one part of the answer is pretty clear. The story found in Acts 8 starts out with Peter and John doing ministry in Samaria. While there, they prayed for new believers to receive the Holy Spirit, but one man suddenly reveals by his request that his heart wasn't right before God. Let's pick up the story from that point.

> When Simon saw that the Spirit was given at the laying on of the apostles' hands, he offered them money and said, "Give me also this ability so that everyone on whom I lay my hands may receive the Holy Spirit." Peter answered: "May your money perish with you, because you thought you could buy the gift of God with money! You have no part or share in this ministry, because your heart is not right before God. Repent of this wickedness and pray to the Lord. Perhaps he will forgive you for having such a thought in your heart. For I see that you are full of bitterness and captive to sin." Then Simon answered, "Pray to the Lord for me so that nothing you have said may happen to me." (Acts 8:18–24)

Apart from all the questions that are raised about what it means for them to pray for believers to receive the Holy Spirit, whether Simon was among those who received the Spirit, or how Peter knew that Simon was full of bitterness and a captive to sin, at least one thing is clear. When someone realizes that they are in the grips of sin, the biblical remedy is always the same: repentance. And with repentance, Simon was told to pray for forgiveness and deliverance from his "captivity" to sin.

Strong, even harsh, words. Not much tenderness or mercy here! Yet, how should we interpret Peter's response? Insensitive? Lacking understanding? Unkind? Notice how Simon responds. He is not offended. He's not crushed. He's not discouraged or hurt. Rather, he immediately accepts the word from Peter as truth, the truth he needed to face and hear, and asks Peter to intercede for him. Repentance is implied, and his request for prayer was the outward sign that he had been convicted of his sin. He now wanted to change as well as avoid whatever horrible consequences might happen if he didn't change.

Repent and pray, that's the biblical model of hope for those who find themselves mired in sin. Not likely to be very popular or deemed to be appropriate by some in a society that so values tolerance, personal freedom, and self-help. Yet, far from being callous or judgmental, Peter's words gave Simon the only way of salvation available.

The chance God's giving us

I'm reminded of a 1994 movie, *Quiz Show*, set in the early days of national television in the United States. Charlie, a contestant on the show, had the longest winning streak ever in the history of the program. He was making a great deal of money as a result. Congress got involved because they suspected that his winning was a sham, and the American public was being deceived. The story, based on a real historical situation and scandals from the 1950s, revolves around the zeal of the congressional investigator, and Charlie's internal angst over his participation in the scam and the increased public scrutiny.

We, the viewers of the movie witness how Charlie, a well-respected Columbia University instructor, is eventually seduced into cheating by slimy, dishonest TV producers who were perpetuating the fraud for illegal monetary gain. As the show goes on, we can feel with him his growing distress over his choices and predicament. The investigator, Dick Goodwin, can't quite catch him; but in their dialogue with one another, Dick keeps trying to coax Charlie to confess—something that would on one hand end Charlie's comfortable life of fame and fortune and lead to disgrace and the loss of his teaching position at Columbia; but, on the other hand, would set him free from the guilt and anguish of living a lie.

One particular interchange has stuck with me for decades. At one point, while passing on the street, the agent presses Charlie once again to come out with the truth. Instead of denying his guilt this time, Charlie, wanting to get Dick off his back, blurts out something like, "Can't you give me a chance?" To which the agent quickly replies, with his thick Bostonian accent, "Charlie, it's a chance I'm giving you."

Pastor Derrick did the right thing to open up to me, confessing his sin and asking for help. None of us can change the past or undo the sins we've committed in our lives, but we can come clean and seek help to turn things around and get back on our feet again. To suggest to someone that they confess their sins and repent is not insensitive or judgmental. It's offering them the only way forward. It's hope.

Sin and the Spirit in battle

Paul's approach to sin was no less intense than Peter's, but he took a different tack. Paul was a teacher and went to great lengths to try to explain to believers that practicing sin and following Christ were exact opposites. Living according to the impulses of sin and following the Spirit were diametrically opposed to one another.

In speaking to the Roman Christians, Paul insists that those who are "baptized into Christ" were baptized into his death for their own salvation and became beneficiaries of Christ's resurrection, meaning they experienced revitalization in this life leading ultimately to their bodily resurrection in the next (Rom 6:3–5). In short, the goal of identifying with Christ through baptism was that they might "live a new life" (Rom 6:4)—now, as well as for eternity. What was to characterize this new life? Paul explained the answer to the Romans in this way:

> The death [Jesus] died, he died to sin once for all; but the life he lives, he lives to God. In the same way, count yourselves dead to sin but alive to God in Christ Jesus. Therefore do not let sin reign in your mortal body so that you obey its evil desires. Do not offer the parts of your body to sin, as instruments of wickedness, but rather offer yourselves to God, as those who have been brought from death to life; and offer the parts of your body to him as instruments of righteousness. For sin shall not be your master, because you are not under law, but under grace. (Rom 6:10–14)

Paul is not speaking here about just believing in Christ's death on behalf of sinners. His teaching to the Romans makes clear that the believer's response to the grace of God in Christ is to be both faith and action. We must believe both that a new reality has been created through the death and resurrection of Christ, and that such faith calls for an appropriate set of concrete actions. In just a few verses, Paul writes at least five imperatives (commands to take action) that we, as those who are in Christ, must take to win the battle against sin:

- Count yourself dead to sin but alive to God in Christ Jesus.

- Do not let sin reign in your mortal body so that you obey its evil desires.

- Do not offer the parts of your body to sin as instruments of wickedness.

- Offer yourselves to God, as those who have been brought from death to life.

- Offer the parts of your body to him, as instruments of righteousness. For sin shall not be your master . . . (Rom 6:11–14a).

If that language is not clear enough, or doesn't get our attention, then we can turn to Colossians, where Paul explicitly instructed his readers: "Put to death, therefore, whatever belongs to your earthly nature: sexual immorality, impurity, lust, evil desires and greed, which is idolatry" (Col 3:5).

"Put to death" is graphic language to indicate how seriously Paul intends followers of Christ to respond to the presence of sin in their lives. In

Galatians, he states the same idea again when he says, "Those who belong to Christ Jesus have crucified the sinful nature with its passions and desires" (Gal 5:24). What this means is that we must come to grips with the seriousness of sin in our lives and take substantial measures to act differently. Paul would tell us today, "Confess your sin, and put a stop to it. Face the truth about how your sin is hurting yourself and others, and undermining your ability to be an instrument of God's love. Stop feeling sorry for yourself and do something about it."

But what exactly is the "something" that we can do that is going to change anything?

Spirit-led repentance

As clear as it is that turning away from sin (repentance) is the consistent biblical mandate, deliverance from the consequences and power of sin is something that requires God's intervention and help. In the New Testament, God's forgiveness and provision for real, lasting change come from a relationship with Jesus Christ and the working of the Holy Spirit.

Every New Testament writer talks about the importance of following Jesus Christ and living one's life for God, but Luke, John, and Paul are the three biblical writers who particularly emphasize the important role of the Holy Spirit as well. Each makes an explicit link between Christ and the Spirit in ways that suggest that those who follow and serve Christ faithfully will be filled and led by the Holy Spirit.

For example, in Luke's version of Jesus' teaching on prayer, Jesus promises the Holy Spirit to seekers: "If you then, though you are evil, know how to give good gifts to your children, how much more will your Father in heaven give the Holy Spirit to those who ask him" (Luke 11:13). John understood Jesus himself as both the "lamb that takes away the sin of the world" and the one who will "baptize with the Holy Spirit" (John 1:29, 33). Paul is the most explicit and detailed about the absolute necessity of drawing on the power of the Holy Spirit to escape the power of sin.

First, in Romans 7, Paul looks back retrospectively on his (or some hypothetical individual's) life before he knew Christ, when, though he wanted to do what was right, he felt a prisoner to sin. He writes:

> So I find this law at work: When I want to do good, evil is right there with me. For in my inner being I delight in God's law; but I see another law at work in the members of my body, waging war

against the law of my mind and making me a prisoner of the law of sin at work within my members. (Rom 7:21–23)

For Paul, sin is the overwhelming, pervasive human problem, and only Jesus Christ and the Holy Spirit can be the solutions. Through Christ, believers find freedom from condemnation for their sins (7:25; 8:1). Through the working of the Holy Spirit, believers are set free from their bondage to sin (8:2). He writes:

> What a wretched man I am! Who will rescue me from this body of death? Thanks be to God—through Jesus Christ our Lord! . . . Therefore, there is now no condemnation for those who are in Christ Jesus. (Rom 7:24—8:1)

> Those who live according to the sinful nature have their minds set on what that nature desires; but those who live in accordance with the Spirit have their minds set on what the Spirit desires. The mind of sinful man is death, but the mind controlled by the Spirit is life and peace; the sinful mind is hostile to God. It does not submit to God's law, nor can it do so. Those controlled by the sinful nature cannot please God. You, however, are controlled not by the sinful nature but by the Spirit, if the Spirit of God lives in you. And if anyone does not have the Spirit of Christ, he does not belong to Christ. But if Christ is in you, your body is dead because of sin, yet your spirit is alive because of righteousness. (Rom 8:5–10)

For Paul, the stakes could not be higher—how we deal with sin in our lives is a matter of life and death, and the difference between pleasing God and not. Yet equally important is a recognition that the key to life is not trying to defeat sin in one's own power. On our own, at best we are limited in our capacity to deal with sin; at worst, we are downright enslaved by it. Only faith in Christ can save us from the condemnation that we deserve. Only the Spirit of God can deliver us from its power. The Spirit won't magically deliver us from the power of sin in most cases, but as we learn to draw on the Spirit for the help we need, more readily and more regularly, we will find more insight, wisdom, and power to fight the daily battles.

Fiery 18th-century spiritual writer, Anglican priest, and mystic William Law went one step further. Not only is the Holy Spirit a needed resource for us to overcome temptation and the power of sin in our lives, Law insisted, but to not draw upon the Spirit is paramount to not truly being in Christ. For Law, no one "can be in the Church [or in Christ] unless he is dead unto sin and alive unto righteousness."[1] That is, we horribly misunderstand the Gospel message—that sinners are saved by grace—if we think that this teaching means that we can be complacent about the sin in our lives or that Christians must be resigned to living under the power of sin. To Law, true followers of Christ should expect to have victory over sin through the power of the Spirit, and doing so was not optional! He explained, "As surely as you must say 'not my will, but thine be done' (Luke 22:42) to become true followers of Christ, so surely you must turn from your own strength to His Spirit to be the doer of His will in you."[2] In other words, Law took Paul's admonishment literally when the latter wrote to the Galatians, "So I say, live by the Spirit, and you will not gratify the desires of the sinful nature" (Gal 5:16).

When we don't feel ready
or able to repent

Yet, as biblically sound as Law's teaching was, sincere Christians often find themselves in exactly the position that Law considers untenable: feeling trapped under the power of sin. Perhaps we don't even know how much control our sinful thinking or behavior is having on us. Perhaps we know very well that we are not where Christ wants us, but we aren't ready to confess our sin, let alone repent of it. Perhaps we want to repent, but we are weary of confessing and asking for forgiveness over and over again, and can't bear the thought of going to God with the same story and pleas for mercy yet one more time. We don't want to give up Christ, and we may even want to be led by the Spirit, but in one area or another, we feel defeated. We are at a wall.

In some cases, we may also be suffering from addiction. Psychiatrist and author of numerous books on Christian spirituality, the late Gerald May, learned from years in psychiatry that all of us are addicts to one thing or another, be it to well-known substances such as alcohol or drugs (what most people think of when they hear the word "addiction"), or to many other substances, processes, or behaviors, such as watching too much television, overeating, indulging in too many desserts, or compulsive sex.[3]

What should we do when we know we should repent, but for whatever reason, it's not happening?

1. Law, *The Power of the Spirit*, 159.
2. Ibid., 169.
3. May, *Addiction & Grace*, 11.

Turn it over to God

When our lives aren't what they should be, and we can't find the inner resources or motivation to change, the Recovery movement has rightly identified that state of being as "powerlessness."[4] When we reach this point in
any area of our lives—whether it is due to an addiction or some hardened
part of our hearts—the solution is not to try harder, by attempting yet once
again to exercise what Richard Rohr calls "heroic willpower."[5] Rather it is to
move in the opposite direction and admit that we cannot change ourselves.
We need to surrender our will to God's.[6] We need to admit our powerlessness to change ourselves and do as every 12-Step Recovery program
instructs: ask God to do in us what we cannot do for ourselves.[7] We don't
have to be alcoholics, or even identify as addicts (though it might actually
be quite helpful for some of us to face reality more honestly in this way), in
order to see the wisdom in this advice. When we have reached the end of
our capacities to change ourselves and all of our strategies have failed us,
turning the problem over to God is both practical and smart.

Acknowledging our powerlessness doesn't mean that we abdicate
our responsibility to make good choices. It means that we admit that we
cannot overcome the power of stubborn sin or addiction on our own. We
need God's power working within us (grace) in order to be released from
the hold addictions have on us. We still have to act responsibly and do
whatever is within our power to do to help ourselves—that is, to access
the resources and power available to us from God and other people, such
as by praying, reading Scripture, seeking counsel, getting therapy, joining
support groups, creating new structures in our lives to reinforce healthier
lifestyle choices, setting better boundaries to keep our distance from temptation, and so forth. We admit our powerlessness not in order to give up
caring about our problem, but to let go of relying exclusively on ourselves to
solve it. We admit our limitations in order to prepare ourselves to reach out
to God for the help we need to make better choices. Dr. May put it this way:

4. Rohr, *Breathing Under Water*, 1–6.

5. Ibid., 24.

6. Ibid., 16–21.

7. Alcoholic Anonymous has simply made famous what the Apostle Paul implied
nearly 2,000 years earlier, when he told the Philippians, "It is God who works in you to
will and to act according to his good purpose" (Phil 2:13).

Addiction cannot be defeated by the human will acting on its own, nor by the human will opting out and turning everything over to divine will. Instead, *the power of grace flows most when human will chooses to act in harmony with divine will. . . .* It is the difference between *testing* God by avoiding one's own responsibilities and *trusting* God as one acts responsibly.[8]

Consequently, when our lives are out of sync with our faith and values, we shouldn't think we should "go away" from God for awhile in order to "figure things out" or until we can "get our act together." On the contrary, no matter how extensive our sin, painful our suffering, complicated our questions, or gnawing our unfulfilled desires, the way forward is by drawing closer to the Spirit, not avoiding or running away from God. The Holy Spirit is the key to knowing and fulfilling God's will for our lives, and the Spirit is essential to helping us work through the moral, spiritual, and deeply personal issues that might be alienating us from God. When we're out of God's will, perhaps feeling confused or lost, or having compartmentalized our lives in such a way that Christ's influence has been shut out of this or that area of our lives, we need divine help to move through the wall.

Jesus said the truth will set us free (John 8:32), and the Holy Spirit is the Spirit of Truth (John 14:17; 16:13; cf. 1 John 4:6). When relying on God's help, we should not expect magical deliverance from our addictions and dependencies, but rather that the Spirit will bring the truth to us in powerful, life-changing ways—often through Scripture, sometimes by circumstances or consequences, and many times in the voices and support of others.

Look for grace in the storm
(Jonah and the whale)

Jonah is perhaps one of the most helpful biblical illustrations of struggling with one's own will versus God's, and of resistance versus surrender. Often when the story is told, preachers will focus on Jonah's rebellion, the distress he brought upon himself and on others who were unfortunately linked to him on the ship to Tarsus, and the big whale that God sent to swallow him up. I would expect that many sermons wind up emphasizing the futility and dangers of resisting God's call and the importance of submission and obedience. All true.

---

8. Ibid., 139.

However, what might not be as evident, but is also extremely important in the story, is *the process* Jonah went through to get back into the will of God. He attempted to flee from God's will by boarding a ship to Tarsus instead of to Nineveh, a graphic metaphor for all the times any of us assert our will over God's. When the storm and waves threatened the ship and the lives of everyone, what did Jonah do? He admitted that he was to blame. Again, another metaphor for the importance of facing reality and confessing our sin. So often, the trouble and suffering we experience in life is brought on by our own choices. Yet, it is our denial and minimizations of our wrongdoing that block our consciences from ringing the alarm bell loudly enough and prevent us from taking needed corrective action. The storm and rolling waves came from the hand of God, but the predicament Jonah was in was of his own making. It wasn't until he admitted his culpability that he was able to take responsibility for his sin and move toward repentance.

Overboard, expecting to drown in the sea, God sends a whale to swallow him. The whale was not a punishment, as awful as it might have been to live in its belly for three days. No, the whale was grace. God saved his life and gave him time to repent. One could assume that God only saved him so that he would fulfill his mission to preach in Nineveh, but why would God care about sinners in Nineveh who needed to repent and not also care about Jonah, who likewise needed to repent?

No, the broader story of Scripture is that God loves us and wants to save us from the consequences of our sin, to free us from our "captivity" to the power of sin, and to lead us to places where we can live fully, love deeply, and give freely through the working of the Spirit in our lives. As Paul says to the Romans, God uses kindness to motivate us to repent (Rom 2:4).

If you feel trapped in the power of sin, or just don't feel ready to confess your sin or to change your ways, ask God to send you a storm and a whale. If just contemplating praying like that doesn't motivate you to repent, ask God to show you whatever you need to see that you've been missing, to clear up your faulty thinking, and to change your heart. As you begin to see inner movement taking place, keep praying until you're free. Ask Christ to take you deeper and deeper into repentance that you might become more and more free—freer to confess, freer to see how harmful your attitude or behavior truly is, freer to say "No" to sin more often, and freer to see how much greater the way of love would be. Ask for a heart that yearns to be back in the sacred love flow, where you can love others genuinely, generously, and graciously.

Ask for the particular grace
you need in the moment

Ignatius of Loyola, the founder of the Jesuits, created a spiritual process to help Christians become more aware of needed changes in their lives and to lean on the grace of God in concrete ways. His Scripture-oriented practice relies heavily on the Spirit for illumination. He advises that practitioners ask God for the grace to receive something specific that God wants to say to them or do in them as they read a Bible passage.

During Ignatian spiritual retreats, participants typically pray for the grace to see something that has been difficult to see, but is critical for developing their relationship with God. They may pray to see the magnitude of God's great love, to see the depth of their sin, to want to choose God above all else, to accept and experience forgiveness, and to hear God's call on their life. When it comes to asking for the Spirit's help with facing and repenting of sin, participants ask for the grace to be grieved by their sin, to be able to repent of it, and to be able to experience real change in their life as a result.

What we need from God at any given point will vary, depending on our state of mind and what we're struggling with. In other words, sometimes the grace we need is to open our eyes to the magnitude of God's love and mercy. Other times, we need to be convicted of sin. Sometimes we need comfort. Sometimes wisdom. Sometimes a powerful word to light a fire under our complacent or resistant bones.

Likewise, the theological message we need will vary depending on our circumstances. Our theology will not change from situation to situation, but what we need to hear at any given moment will. Sometimes, we need to hear that God is loving, merciful, and good. Other times, it's thinking about God's holiness, wrath, and justice that will move us. Sometimes, only a message of God's unconditional love and our utter dependence on him will provide the rest and relief we need to forgive ourselves and get back on our feet again. Other times, it will take a sermon on human accountability before God and a call to be "good and faithful servants" to motivate us. Accordingly, we need to reach out for teaching and guidance that will bring the word of God to us that we need in our present circumstances. We may even want to seek out different theologians or preachers at various times in our lives, providing the messages we hear or read are biblically sound and empowered by the Spirit. Again, our goal should not necessarily be to change our theology (though sometimes that is exactly what is needed), but to draw on the particular emphases or perspectives that different writers or speakers may be able to offer us, which God will use to help us at this time.

Rather than search for the one "true" or "best" theological voice to guide me, I try to expose myself to many different voices, from different theological schools of thought, expecting none to have the whole truth, but all to have something to contribute to my way of thinking. All theologians are motivated and influenced by something in their own lives and broader contexts as well as their intellectual and rational analysis of Scripture. Their "contexts" shape their interpretations and fuel their particular emphases. This phenomenon is not a bad thing, nor does it necessarily produce bad theology. It can actually be quite helpful, providing that we recognize the bias for what it is and isn't. "Contextualized" interpretation of Scripture, and thus contextualized teaching and preaching, isn't (or rarely is) the "whole" truth on any given point, but it is (or can be) a meaningful interpretation for the context in which the teaching or sermon is given. In my particular time of need, some theologians and preachers will be better able to speak into my life than others. At another time, I will reach for a different book on my shelf.

For example, as mentioned earlier, Willian Law represents one end of the theological spectrum in his insistence that true Christians must and will have victory over sin if they are truly in Christ. Catholics teach that God's grace restores us to an Adam/Eve–like state, where we can once again act righteously, and are responsible to do so. Martin Luther, on the other hand, taught that those in Christ cannot not sin, but are still saved by God's grace and through faith in what Christ did on their behalf. Thus, he insisted that Christians are and always will be "simultaneously saints and sinners."[9] Each theological position is well-grounded in Scripture, but springs from different contextual issues and concerns.

Luther was grappling with his own sense of guilt and unworthiness, fostered and perpetuated by Catholic teaching in his day. His emphasis on grace alone through faith in Jesus Christ alleviated his angst over the sin in his life that he could not eliminate. Two centuries later, however, William Law was reacting to the opposite problem. In Law's day, preachers were so resigned to the reality of sin in each person's life that they neither offered

---

9. Luther's classic theological formulation often appears in Latin: *simul justus et peccator*.

hope for change nor taught people to call upon the Spirit's power to resist temptation and to free themselves from the bondage of living in sin. Their different contexts did not change Scripture, but they greatly affected the formulation of their theology, their dialogue with other theologians, and their preaching for ordinary Christians.

Personally, I have needed to hear both extreme messages at different points in my life. One time in particular, I felt so discouraged about my own failures and sin that only the message of God's unconditional love and acceptance could lift me up and set me free from my despair and (over) reliance on myself.[10] At others times, when I've been complacent or even resistant to the Spirit, I've needed a good jolt of conviction and challenge to wake me up and put my life in better order again. To put it in more traditional language, I needed to repent of my sin—face the truth, feel remorse, confess it, renounce it, and turn away from it.[11]

Though the call to listen to and cooperate with the Spirit may sound like a responsibility we have to shoulder on our own, it's not. The truth is, all spiritual growth in our lives actually flows out of the grace of God through what Christ did on our behalf on the cross and through the Holy Spirit's working in our hearts and minds. When we feel as if we simply can't do what the Holy Spirit is asking of us, we don't know what to do, or we feel inadequate or powerless, we need to go back to God for help. We need to ask for the particular grace we need to be able to change what we cannot

10. See *The Spirit-Led Leader*, 193–5, where I tell the story of when I experienced the love and grace of God in a powerful, life-changing way. I was a seminary graduate, a pastor for several years, and had just earned a PhD in New Testament studies. Yet, unable to find a suitable job and having to face my own sense of failure to live up to my own standards as a follower of Christ, I was at a real low. However, unexpectedly, I was given the opportunity to attend a week long seminar on shame and grace. The first night my own false basis for self-esteem was exposed and the message of God's acceptance of and love for me, the Father's child, whom Christ died to save, struck home in a way it never had before. Even though I had preached numerous sermons and given countless teachings on the Gospel, it took a string of disappointments and a sense of failure for me to finally let go of relying on my ability to achieve and perform in order to feel secure and valued. The experience was a turning point in my relationship with God, how I viewed myself, and how I view and relate to others. Now, instead of focusing so much on their performance or status, I feel much more free to see others as God sees them—dearly loved and valued.

11. In *One Step at a Time*, I talk about the importance of facing reality and coming to grips with needed changes in our lives. My family's walk across northern Spain on the *camino* was grueling at times, but forced me to see more clearly the extent of my own selfishness and sinful attitudes that were hurting my relationships with my wife and sons. Facing reality, seeking inner change, and seeking the help of the Spirit are critical on the spiritual journey. See, especially chapter 8, "Crossing Bridges" (179–99).

change on our own. Then, as we experience the Spirit at work in us, cleansing us and providing new strength, we will gain greater assurance that God has forgiven us and still has good for us to do, no matter how far we have fallen or how much we have struggled with sin and failed in the past.

Conclusion

The old saying that I first heard as a child, whose original source I do not know, is still true: "God loves us as we are, but loves us too much to leave us as we are." God's grace is indeed big enough to surround us with love and kindness, even when we are mired in sin at times. But we dare not become complacent. We must not take God's kindness for granted and miss out on the ways God wants to change us and use us for good in the world. We are foolish if we fail to reach out for the help that is available to us. We will be needlessly paralyzed by a false sense of powerlessness if we do not stand up against evil in the name and power of Jesus.

Theologians differ on how they believe God's grace works in human lives and the extent to which they believe real transformation is possible. Yet, all agree that God has given us a high standard for holiness and righteousness, that sin is a destructive force in our lives and in our relationship with God, and that only God's grace can save us. While some traditions are more optimistic about human capacity for living righteously and lovingly, with God's help; and others insist that we must accept that we cannot not sin and must rely entirely on God's grace for salvation; all agree that we must take sin and grace seriously. Practically, our ability to live in the sacred love flow and keep in step with the Spirit depends on our doing so.

Your next Spirit-led steps

What is the Spirit saying to you right now? If you were to take sin and grace more seriously in your life, how would you think differently? What would you do differently? How would you pray differently? What help would you seek out from the Spirit and from others—pastors, professional counselors, recovery groups, accountability partners, and other trusted friends and mentors? Journal with these questions and make a concrete plan for something you can and will do differently this week. Enlist someone to help you to take sin and grace more seriously in your life, so that you can live in the sacred love flow more fully and consistently.

9

Be God-Confident

I can do everything through him who gives me strength.

PHILIPPIANS 4:13

"IT COMES UP SIX times day." "Jerry" is almost beside himself. "It's every-where! Every time I lose control, I feel uncomfortable. I get emotional. I get angry. I feel depressed. Sometimes, I just can't get out of my emotional state.

"Take this morning for example. My 10 a.m. meeting with my pro-spective client did not go well. This guy was basically calling me a liar. If our sales manager hadn't jumped in to help bail me out I don't know what I would have done. This is the second time he has attacked me.

"I was so upset. As the two of them were talking, I suddenly remem-bered to pray. I realized, I'm not upset that he called me a liar. I'm not upset that we might not get this deal. I'm upset because the situation was out of control. When I feel that I can't control a situation, I lose it. I can't stand it, and the situation brings out my worst."

When Jerry entered spiritual life coaching, his main goal was to rise to the next level of leadership. He already made a nice six-figure salary, was widely respected in his church, and had a gift for public speaking. Surely, it must be time to take his career to the next level!

However, it wasn't long before he began to see that he wasn't ready to go to the next level. Sure, he could probably find new ways to make a lot of money. He could get bigger speaking gigs. Yet, he was trying to do it all on his own, in his own strength. When everything went well, he felt like a million dollars, on top of the world. But when things felt out of control, he would crumble or lash out. What Jerry lacked was not more opportunity or ability. He lacked spiritual tools to handle feeling out of control. He wasn't ready to go to the next level of Christian leadership, because he needed to learn how to let the Holy Spirit lead and guide in the midst of daily life. He needed to become a whole lot more comfortable trusting God when he wasn't on stage or making a big sale, and in all those times when things weren't going the way he wanted.

As Jerry learned to lean on God more, his perspective changed and his ability to handle stressful situations improved. Looking back on his experience with the angry prospective client, Jerry remarked, "Thanks to the intervention of my sales manager who bought me some time, and to the Holy Spirit, I started praying. Right there in the middle of the conversation, I asked God for help to know what to do. As soon as I did, I heard God say, 'Just listen. I will show you when to jump back in.' Sure enough, as my peace returned, the time for me to rejoin the conversation came naturally. I didn't lose my cool, and was able to respond to the prospective client appropriately.

"I don't know if we'll close the deal, but this experience confirmed everything we have been talking about. When I feel out of control, I feel uncomfortable. I start to get down on myself. I start reacting to people and try to get control of everything and everyone. If I can just slow down, I realize [all this negativity about myself] is all in my head. It's not up to me to get control of the situation. I have to remember that God is in control and focus on reconnecting with him."

Staying Connected

Like Jerry, a strong, hardworking Christian leader, who was nonetheless being discombobulated by circumstances outside of his control, we, too, can suddenly fall out of step with the Spirit due to our reactions to some disturbing situation in our life. Our inner felt need for control, for example, surges forward and takes over, and we stop listening to the Spirit and drawing on God's help to handle the situation well. What we need to do instead is to do all we can to stay connected to the Spirit, or, when we realize that we've lost our connection, to re-establish a conscious connection with God and ask for help. We need to seek a healthy and faith-full perspective that is built on trusting God and approaching the situation with wisdom, inner strength, and confidence that come from the Spirit.

Practically, this often begins by relinquishing our anxiety to God in prayer, and asking God to work in us, through us, and in the situation for good. It is not the prayer itself that produces the inner peace and confident perspective that we need, as if it were a magic incantation. No, our relief and help come from the Holy Spirit, who is already present within us, but whom we are accessing in a conscious way by praying. This process of keeping in step with the Spirit when we are most vulnerable to falling back on our own instincts or to being overwhelmed by our fears is exactly what Paul advised the Philippians to use. When they were anxious over the threat of persecution from nonbelievers in Philippi and were in turmoil due to internal conflicts within the church, he wrote:

> Do not be anxious about anything, but in everything, by prayer and petition, with thanksgiving, present your requests to God. And the peace of God, which transcends all understanding, will guard your hearts and your minds in Christ Jesus. (Phil 4:6–7)

Paul doesn't speak specifically about being filled with the Spirit or led by the Spirit in his letter to the Philippians, as he does extensively in Romans and Galatians. Instead, in this context, he speaks more broadly about God as the one is actively at work in the life of believers, whose power and peace come to those who rely on him and seek him out in prayer.[1] Throughout the letter, he repeatedly speaks of the importance of focusing our minds on God, Christ, Christlike values in the body of Christ, our calling and so forth, ultimately with the goal of having the "same mind [in us] that was in Christ Jesus" (Phil 2:5, NRSV).[2]

Regardless of Paul's decision not to speak of God's activity in our lives in Philippians and Colossians the same way he does in Romans and Galatians (by referencing the Holy Spirit explicitly), the basic message is the same: "it is God who works in you to will and to act according to his good purpose" (Phil 2:13). Our part is to reach out to God consciously, so that we can focus our mind as well as our heart on what the Spirit is doing in us and how the Spirit may want to lead us. How we focus our minds makes all the difference in the world to our ability to keep in step with the Spirit, which means, practically, being able to draw on the mind of Christ and the power

---

1. E.g., Phil 1:6; 19; 2:12–13; 3:8–9; 4:19.

2. There are many references in Philippians to the importance of what and how we think, and to seeking God's help to shape our thinking so that it will be in better sync with Christ and God's will for the church (e.g., Phil 1:9–11; 2:2–9; 3:3–15).

of God in order to live with more wisdom, strength, peace, confidence, and love in the midst of challenging circumstances.[3]

Toward the end of the letter, Paul reiterates the connection between how we focus our minds and our experience of God within us when he writes:

> Finally, brothers [and sisters], whatever is true, whatever is noble, whatever is right, whatever is pure, whatever is lovely, whatever is admirable—if anything is excellent or praiseworthy—think about such things. Whatever you have learned or received or heard from me, or seen in me—put it into practice. And the God of peace will be with you. (Phil 4:8–9)

As Craig Keener rightly observes, "The mind's focus here in Philippians 4:8 is a world away from Romans 7 [the mind in slavery to the desires of the flesh], resembling instead the mind of the Spirit (Rom 8:6) and the mind of Christ (1 Cor 2:16)."[4]

Remember God is for you

Sometimes, we fall out of step with the Spirit, not because we are overtaken by our emotions and swept away by our need to be in control, but because of the Adam-and-Eve-in-the-garden syndrome. We feel too ashamed or unworthy of God's help, so we hide from God. Our own guilt and shame might make us afraid to open up to God. We may fear that God is going to come down on us or tell us to do something we don't want to do. As a result, we may lack peace and confidence either because we are going it alone or because we are afraid of getting too close to God.

What's the alternative? Trust that God is good, does care, is for you, not against you, and will help you to get wherever you need to be. Go to God even if, or especially if, you are afraid of the encounter. Ask the Spirit to speak to you, give you an image, or create a feeling within you to help you regain perspective and return to equilibrium so that you can confidently step forward in sync with the Spirit again.

---

3. For Keener, following the Spirit has everything to do with how and on what we focus our minds. See, e.g., his discussion of key passages in Philippians and Colossians that illustrate "Paul's approach to transformed thinking," the subtitle of his book (Keener, *The Mind of the Spirit*, 217–55).

4. Ibid., 229.

An unexpected answer to prayer

One spring, on an Ignatian spiritual retreat in central France, I was praying with the assigned Scripture text, John 21:15–20. For years, every time I
read the verses where Jesus asks Peter if he loves him and tells him to feed
his sheep, I would feel this surge of emotion. I kept wondering if God was
calling me back into the pastoral ministry that I left decades ago in favor of
pursuing a teaching ministry.

It was painful to read this text, because I always felt like somehow I
was out of God's will without any way to make things right. I had turned
a corner vocationally. I had many new commitments and responsibilities.
Going back to the pastorate was not a realistic option for me, yet every
time I read this text, I felt horrible. If God was calling me to go back to the
pastorate, how in the world could I possibly comply?

However, this time when I read it, I was in for a surprise. After unsuc-
cessfully trying to get out of the exercise, I submitted myself to listen to
whatever the Holy Spirit wanted to tell me. Not surprisingly, as soon as I
read Jesus' words, "Do you love me? . . . [Then] feed my sheep," I felt the
same pain I always feel. Yet this time, I realized that what I was feeling was
not a calling, but guilt. Not guilt for ignoring God's call, but unresolved
pain from something that happened back in 1988.

Though it had been more than twenty-five years, I was still feeling
guilty about how I left my first church. I had been a pastor for four years
and had worked out a deal whereby I could start my doctoral work. My
hours at the church would be reduced, and my wife's would be increased.
However, when our second child was born prematurely, it became clear
that she could not increase her hours and would in fact have to decrease
them.

Since there was no way I could handle full time at the church and in
a PhD program, I decided to resign. The decision was a bit rushed, and I
didn't allow enough time to search for creative solutions with the congregation. But the most troubling part of the decision I made is what happened
after I left.

What I didn't anticipate was how much the church would suffer because of my rather sudden departure, and how difficult it would be for
them to find a new pastor. For more than two decades, I had been carrying
around a lot of guilt for what happened, and in that moment of listening to
the Spirit, I suddenly knew what I needed to do.

I needed to ask for forgiveness. I needed to ask God to forgive me for being too immature and inexperienced to know how my decision would affect the church, my wife, and me. Instead of trying to justify myself or excuse myself, I needed to simply accept my part in causing other people pain and confess it to God.

You might think, "Well, you shouldn't be so hard on yourself or take so much responsibility for what happened after you left. Besides you were so young, how could you have known everything you know now?" Perhaps so, but what I needed for my own spiritual and psychological healing was not to minimize my responsibility. Rather, I needed to honestly face my own contribution to the suffering of others, seek God's forgiveness, and then forgive myself.

When I was willing to listen to the Spirit, my thinking was straightened out. I wasn't being called back into the pastorate, I needed resolution over my leaving a former church. As I yielded my will to cooperate with the Spirit's leading by seeking forgiveness, I suddenly felt a great deal of peace.

What a surprise. What a gift. I finally felt freedom to let go of what I could not change from the past, and freer to focus on the teaching ministry that God had given me in the present. My unresolved guilt and shame had been undermining my confidence in myself, and ironically, my confidence in God as well. When I realized that God could be trusted with the pain I was carrying, I experienced both a resurgence of trust both in God and in God's call on my life.

In encouraging the Roman Christians, who were apparently suffering from persecution for their faith, the Apostle Paul reminded them of God's unwavering commitment to their well-being and their unbreakable bond to Christ. He assures them that, because God "works for the good of those who love him, who have been called according to his purpose," they can be confident in God (Rom 8:28). "If God is for us, who can be against us?" he asks rhetorically (Rom 8:31). No matter who may accuse us or attack us, or what evil may come upon us, Paul goes on to say, "I am convinced that neither death nor life, neither angels nor demons, neither the present nor the future, nor any powers, neither height nor depth, nor anything else in all creation, will be able to separate us from the love of God that is in Christ Jesus our Lord" (Rom 8:38–39).

The secret to living with confidence is not rooted in our abilities to create security for ourselves, to always make good decisions, to perform well in every situation, or to achieve great things. Confidence for daily life and all life's challenges comes from believing that God is actively at work in our lives for good. God is for us, not against us. As we stay immersed in the sacred love flow, believing that nothing can separate us from God's love, we realize we have an eternal basis for confidence to help us through the darkest and toughest moments. Staying consciously connected to the promise and presence of God's love provides the kind of perspective we need to face our trials with faith and hope.

The kind of personal and trusting connection to God that we're talking about here also helps us to believe that God is actively helping others in the midst of their suffering as well. My experiences working with survivors in some of the most difficult places on the globe has taught me the latter point in ways I didn't expect.

God spottings

As I listened to Rwandan genocide survivor Sakindi's story and saw what he and his sisters had to endure, [5] I was first shocked, then angry, and then sad. Where was God for them and for all the others victims of violence? My distress only intensified when I found out that some 85 percent of Rwandans identified as Christian before the 1994 genocide. Yet church members turned against their fellow church members and neighbors. Even some clergy participated in the killing. In a few particularly egregious circumstances, pastors locked their own parishioners in their church before bulldozing it, setting it on fire, or turning them over to the *génocidaires*.

I wasn't surprised to learn that some survivors of genocide felt that God had abandoned them in their dark hour. I wasn't shocked to hear some victims of violence admit to losing their faith in God and humanity. And I could not criticize anyone suffering from such horrors for wanting to die. Yet that's not how everyone responded or responds to suffering, and not how everyone thinks. Not by a long shot.

I needed a genocide survivor like Sakindi to help me see what I was missing. The insight came to me when he showed us his new house that some foreigners had purchased for him. I was struck by how thankful he was. Never mind that the house was still uninhabitable at the time. He couldn't afford the sheet metal to repair the holes in the roof, and didn't have the money to replace the over-filled latrine behind the house. Never mind that there was no kitchen, and the walls of one of the three small

5. See chapter 7 above.

rooms was about to collapse. From his perspective, even if he had to go without food for a couple of days from time to time, he felt so grateful just having a home that he could call his own and offer to his sisters. As he stood in front of his house, beaming with pride and joy, he was not thinking about all that he had to endure in the past. I saw that what mattered to him was the gift of the moment, and his hope for the future.

I, the outsider, materially affluent, highly educated, privileged in countless ways, was angry at God on his behalf. Yet, he, who had hardly any possessions, periodically lacked food, and had to try to cope with responsibilities and needs that made him physically sick at times from stress, was thankful to God for his blessings. And on this day, in particular, he was very grateful to God for showing his love and generosity to his sisters and him through the gift of his new home and new "parents."

As I saw his face and listened to him talk, I suddenly realized something I had been totally missing. God had not abandoned Sakindi as I had assumed. I just couldn't see God until I followed the impulse of love and acted on the compassion I felt. I couldn't see God until I started looking for God within myself and in others, when we are at our best rather than at our worst.

In that single moment, something shifted within me. I stopped looking in vain for signs of God "out there" somewhere, independent of ordinary human beings. Instead, I started seeing God where God has been and is—in Sakindi's uncle who saved his life, in those who gave his sisters and him something to eat when they were starving, and in the man who took them in before he died. I began to see God in Béatrice, the woman who gave him a job for years so that he could afford to pay his rent, and who offered him whatever she could, though she had limited resources and so many others to care for.

Sakindi sees God in all the faces, voices, arms, and hands of each person who has helped his sisters and him over the years. He also sees God now in my wife, Jill, and me. And because he sees God in us, it is suddenly easier for me to see God in myself as well as in him.

In the inspiration of the moment, I went from questioning whether God is truly anywhere to seeing God everywhere. The darkness may be great, but when Christ shines through you and me, the light is greater.

> For God, who said, "Let light shine out of darkness," made his light shine in our hearts to give us the light of the knowledge of the glory of God in the face of Christ. But we have this treasure in jars

of clay to show that this all-surpassing power is from God and not from us. (2 Cor 4:6–7)

Wherever I see good, I now see God. Whenever I do good, I assume God is at work. As William Law observed, "Every stirring with the heart of man towards good is but the voice of Christ by His Holy Spirit calling, 'Follow me' (Matt 4:19)."[6] Spirit-led followers of Christ are those in whom "God . . . works . . . to will and to act according to his good purpose," (Phil 2:13). "For we are God's workmanship, created in Christ Jesus to do good works, which God prepared in advance for us to do" (Eph 2:10).

Self-confident or God-confident?

I had to laugh. I was walking on the 40-foot-by-40-foot labyrinth in the Chartres Cathedral, praying for inspiration and peace. I was trying to get motivated to write an essay for my blog site on self-confidence. Instead, I just felt anxious about whether I really had anything worth saying!

Whenever I lack self-confidence like this, or become overly self-conscious, I tend to freeze up or become horribly awkward. I'm afraid I won't be clever, interesting, or original enough, and my readers won't keep reading or won't respect me. So, I procrastinate.

This kind of paralyzing self-consciousness and lack of self-confidence is widespread in my experience. Many of my spiritual life coaching clients, students, and friends wrestle with these same issues in their own ways. As far as I can tell, the root cause of the problem is often fear. Fear of failure, fear of rejection, fear of looking foolish, fear of what others may be thinking or feeling about us.[7] Our confidence falters, and we hesitate to put ourselves forward.

Sometimes, we have the opposite problem, too. Driven by pride, we become determined to prove our worth or superiority to others—or to ourselves. We may accomplish a lot, but too often the end result is more about us, and less about God. At the same time, pride can be the cause of a low self-image and our feeling badly ourselves. It works like this: when we can't do something as well as we'd like, our pride can't bear the thought of our

---

6. Law, *The Power of the Spirit*, 168.

7. Cf. McGee, *Search for Significance*. McGee argues that all human fears, at least in social relationships as well as in many other areas of life, can be boiled down to four main fears: fear of failure, fear of rejection, fear of being blamed, and fear of shame.

"losing" or "not measuring up." So we mope about or feel embarrassed over our shortcomings and failures, and sometimes even stop trying.

Either way—puffed up into self-serving overdrive or deflated into self-defeating under-drive—we can easily become too pre-occupied with Self. What's needed instead is a shift in our focus. We need to move from being so self-conscious (worrying about our performance or what others might be thinking about us) to being more God-conscious (focusing on what God wants for our lives and how the Holy Spirit works through imperfect mortals to bless others). And what a difference it makes!

Keeping in step with the Spirit is not mysterious. Nor is the secret to self-confidence hidden from the followers of Christ. At core to both keeping in step with the Spirit and self-confidence is simply trusting that God is actively at work in our lives, leading and guiding us in ways that fit with God's good purposes for each of us and those whose lives we touch. The more confident we are in God and the Spirit's working in our lives, the more confident we will be in ourselves—for the right reasons and on the right basis. The more confident we are, the more peace, strength, courage, and motivation we will feel to carry on with the good work God has called us to do.

When I become more God-confident at least five things happen:

1. I am more likely to base my self-image primarily on how God looks at me (I am loved, valued, cherished, and forgiven; and have purpose in life), rather than putting so much weight on the fickle opinions of others or on my ability to impress them. I start focusing on what God will do through me, and stop being so preoccupied with myself and my own image.

2. I focus on how I might best serve Christ's purposes today to meet the needs of those God brings into my life. I trust that God has specific work for me to do (Eph 2:10) and that I have been made uniquely with a unique mission in the world. I focus on serving rather than on what I might get out of the experience or on how my accomplishments could advance my reputation or status.[8]

---

8. See Crabb, *Connecting*, 103–26. Cf., Geoffrion, *The Spirit-Led Leader,* 91–93, where I briefly discuss Crabb's four ways that leaders tend to serve themselves rather than Christ in their leadership roles. Aligning our will with God's will includes continually subordinating our personal agendas to whatever will best serve Christ.

3. I stop procrastinating, because I know I have important work to do in the name of Jesus, service that means a lot to me personally and stems from God's calling and will. Rather than waiting until I feel like getting started or I am certain of "success," I press forward out of commitment and faith.

4. I work harder to offer my best to God, because I feel so grateful to be loved by God and eager to be part of whatever the Holy Spirit is doing. Rather than feel as if I have to work hard to earn God's love, I let my thankful heart lead me into service.

5. I make a conscious decision to trust that God will do good things through me. Rather than think that "success" all depends on me, the perfection of the product I create, or my delivery of my sermon or teaching, I place my confidence in what God will do when I use my spiritual gifts or reach out in love. I certainly will work hard, prepare well, and try to do a good job, but I will replace the performance anxiety that sometimes feels crippling and the worries about what kind of reception I'm going to get with confidence in what God will do.

In short, focusing on self either keeps us from getting to the work God has for us to do, or distorts our motivation and message by seeking gratification or glory for ourselves. Focusing on God makes our confidence soar and motivates us to get going with the good work God has for us to do—today.

Keeping up our God-confidence

In truth, the path of the Spirit is pretty well marked out for each of us— certainly not all the particular details, but the character, the spirit, and the intention of God's ways are well known through Scripture. Once again, the way of God is the way of love. When we don't know what else to do, choosing a loving action is likely to be close if not right on target for most situations. Practical Christian living often comes down to consciously reminding ourselves of what we already know to be true, and then acting on it in the ways available to us.

Yet, staying in this place of God-confidence takes effort.

As we proceed along the Spirit-led path, we can so easily get distracted, especially by our reactions to people whom we let disturb, entice, annoy, consume, intimidate, threaten, or otherwise drag us out of the sacred love flow. On any given day, I can get swept away by negative or strong emotions, forgetting what I'm doing or should be focusing on. For example, I may be writing, helping my family, or working on an important work project, when suddenly some memory pops into my head and I get flooded with some unwanted emotions. I may start rehearsing in my mind how someone hurt me or fantasizing about getting revenge. I may make some short-sighted lifestyle decision that dissipates my energy or threatens my health. I might suddenly bite someone's head off when only moments before I was feeling love toward someone else. I may start a less important project leaving the more important one unfinished. I may hesitate on following through on a commitment because I start second-guessing myself or doubting God.

We're all going to get off track at times. It is easy to get distracted from our core values, faith, and priorities. It's quite normal to miss the Spirit's leading on occasion, waste time and resources, or actually veer off into trouble. Perfection is not attainable in this life. Yet, we must not underestimate the cost of drifting away from the Spirit. All wayward paths can seriously undermine our confidence in God and in ourselves as servants of Christ.

What can we do? First, we can try to minimize the number of times we yield to the wayward impulses. If we take time to reflect on our life experience and identify all the ways we tend to go wrong, we will more readily recognize when we are starting down a wrong path and be better able to stop ourselves more quickly. When self-awareness and willpower don't work, and we find ourselves sucked into a negative attitude or mired in a misguided course of action, we need to consciously reach out to reconnect with God and ask for help.

To this end, my former spiritual director, the late John Ackerman, taught me a helpful spiritual practice that can be applied in many different circumstances, including whenever we discover that we have moved away from the Spirit's leading. At such times, the best thing to do is to "stop, look, and listen." Stop whatever you're doing. Look at what's going on and what's going to happen if you stay on the course you're on. And listen to whatever the Spirit may be saying to you, possibly to show you the way forward or to simply redirect your attention to something far more constructive and loving.

We may need to step back to get our bearings, but once we have regained perspective, courage, and strength to do what God is calling us to do, it's time step back into the flow confidently. The longer we delay, the farther we move away from the Spirit's leading, and the greater the power of the wrong path. The sooner we catch ourselves (or the Spirit brings the problem to our attention), and take corrective action to rejoin the Spirit in the sacred love flow, the better.

To stay on the path, it's usually helpful to coach ourselves through the inhibiting emotions, doubts, or distractions. We can use self-talk to get over the emotional hurdles by telling ourselves things like, "Yes, this task is scary or hard, but I need to do it." "I feel inadequate, but God has called me to this. I will get started out of obedience." "I may never be 100% sure of God's will, but I'm going to do *something*, trusting God to guide me to wherever Christ wants me to be." Our emotional responses may be involuntary, but we can catch ourselves when we're getting swept away in them and ask, "Is this how I want to react?" "What does the Rule of Love call for here?" "What would acting in faith look like in this situation?" "If I were truly to be God-confident, what would I do next?"

Conclusion

Our life paths are going to keep winding back and forth over the years, shifting direction from time to time. We are going to explore, experiment, learn, re-learn, seek, question, and attempt to follow our hearts, minds, and convictions in a wide variety of contexts. Such exploration in life is normal and necessary to help us learn more about ourselves, where we thrive, and where we have the most to contribute. At times, the turns we make may be Spirit-led. At other times, they may be prompted from ignorance or misguided attempts to find our way. Yet, no matter what the reason, except when our motivation clearly comes from selfishness or our sinful desires, as followers of Christ we must trust that God will lead and guide the steps we take in faith.

Without knowing where each turn will take us, we may act confidently, trusting that ultimately God will direct us and teach us through the choices we make, whether or not they were wise and good decisions at the time. Even if we discover later that our course of action was way off base for who we are or for our callings, God can still redeem our failures and mistakes, and re-direct us from that place. Confidence in God means stepping out in faith to do what seems best at the time, trusting that no matter what happens God can still work through us wherever we choose to go and then can lead us to a better place from there.

It doesn't matter how many times we twist and turn in life. What matters is that the path we are on is Spirit-led—and that we get back to the Spirit-led path as quickly as possible when we stray from it. Yet on our own we do not have the power to change our most deep-seated instincts and habits. God has to do the deep inner work to set us free and to keep us on the Spirit-led path. Our part is to stay connected to the Spirit, to keep re-ordering our thinking by biblical values and teaching, and to not lose heart to start again when we've failed or missed the Spirit's promptings. We need to focus on keeping in step with the Spirit on the path that leads to God,[9] rather than on trying to change ourselves or others in our own strength for our own self-serving purposes. The needed changes in our lives must flow from the Spirit's activity in us and others, in God's timing and in God's way.

Faith is a gift from God, but to walk by faith is a choice. Acting in confidence means trusting that the Spirit will show us what most needs to be done, in spite of our limitations, failures, and emotional turbulence, and will often give us the right perspective when we ask for help and listen. When I'm feeling shaky or lacking confidence at the beginning of a day or project, I often pray, "Lord, I'm going to trust you. Please work in me and in this situation in ways that best fit with your good purposes." Then, I step forward trusting that the Spirit will lead and guide me along the way, however long and winding the road may be. As for the outcome and fruit of my work, I leave that in God's hands.

Your next Spirit-led steps

Isaiah said, speaking to the LORD, "You will keep in perfect peace him [or her] whose mind is steadfast, because he [or she] trusts in you" (Isaiah 26:3). Choosing to trust God in every aspect of your life and focusing on the Spirit-led path before you is what a steadfast mind is all about. When you feel yourself starting to veer off the path in your mind, heart or behavior, try simply saying to yourself, "Stay on the path. Stay on the path." As

---

9. The Spirit-led life is both walking with God and journeying toward God simultaneously. We have Christ already in us and yet we must continually seek to become "perfect" (Gk, *teleios*, "complete") in him over time (Col 1:27–29). "Completeness" in Christ is not perfectionism or getting everything right all the time, it's increasingly fusing Christ's identity with ours. It's seeking to know Christ more and more, and increasingly giving up our own wills and desires in order that Christ may dwell in us more fully and may shine through us more clearly and brilliantly. See, too, Phil 3:7–14.

your mind and spirit obey your instructions, you will feel the temptations diminish in power and the peace within you deepen and strengthen.

Reflect on how your life would be different if you were more God-confident, especially during those times when you feel out of control, feel inadequate, or, conversely, tend to rely on yourself too much. Write down your thoughts in your spiritual journal or share them with a trusted friend or spiritual mentor. Identify some specific areas in your life that you need to put into God's hands right now . . . and then do it.

10

Keep the Faith

Why are you downcast, O my soul?
Why so disturbed within me?

Put your hope in God, for I will yet
praise him, my Savior and my God.

Psalm 42:5

In response to a *Huffington Post* article I once published, entitled "When Prayer Makes a Difference in Suffering," a number of atheists responded angrily and attempted to refute my argument for putting faith in God. One in particular expressed her objections this way:

> The thing is religion sellers get you coming and going. If you pray for God to help you in a crisis and the crisis goes away . . . all praise to God. If you pray for help and the crisis doesn't go away He has different plans for you or He never gives you more than you can handle. So ante up. The religion sellers win both ways. BTW [By the way], why would a just and loving God give you pain to teach you a lesson? I'll stick to the facts of the world . . . sh*t happens, good things happen, randomly. (Thinkingwomanmillstone, 6/9/10)[1]

Faith and disbelief. Two perspectives. Two very different worldviews. One claims that God's intimate involvement in our lives is a fact. The other, God's help is a fiction. To someone who is frustrated or disillusioned with

---

1. To read the original Huffington Post article that prompted this and other responses from bloggers, see Geoffrion, "When Prayer Makes a Difference."

God, believers may seem out of touch with reality, at best, and dishonest or devious, at worst. Those who believe in God, trust in Christ, and rely on biblical teaching for guidance have just the opposite point of view. To believers, the Christian faith helps to make sense of life and opens the door to greater meaning and purpose in relationship with God. And it's those who insist that God does not exist or doesn't care about us who are out of touch with reality, at best, and seriously blind, misguided or deceived, at worst.

When we start from an assumption that God is real and answers prayer, our seemingly random experiences don't seem so random anymore. The unpredictable nature of God's response (or lack thereof) to our requests may still confound us at times, but we can often find God at work in both the "yeses" and "no's" to our prayers. And while we may suffer greatly from any number of painful experiences, through eyes of faith we see the good that can come out of even the most tragic situations. These experiences are not proofs for God, but rather provide encouragement for many who already have faith to continue believing.

If, on the other hand, we let the perplexing mysteries of God, the seeming randomness of life, and the horrors of human suffering undermine our faith, we lose something vital to our well-being. The light has not come on, as skeptics might claim, but has gone out. We've not "grown up," we've given up. When we should have been wrestling with God for deeper understanding and personal growth, having been humbled at the wall, finally ready to learn something about ourselves and about our need for God that had not been possible before, we abandon the quest. Jesus said it is those who seek who find (Matt 7:7), and we've stopped seeking. We may think that we have reached a new height of understanding, but those who know and love God perceive that we've fallen into a dark hole.

You, as a reader of this book, may feel that you are nowhere near where these disbelievers have gone. However, in the face of real life questions and suffering, you may be more in danger of joining them than you think, even if to a much lesser degree. Many of those I've met or who have written to me were once believers in Christ, but they've been hurt. They're angry. They've become cynical. They're often arrogant and defiant. And they've turned their back on God and Christ. While this may not describe you well at all, you may still be struggling with your faith in ways that are detrimental to your relationship with God and your ability to say "yes" wholeheartedly. The wind may have gone out of your sails. You may still be seeking, asking, and knocking, but the niggling doubts or the buried resentments have been holding you back. Your "yes" to God may have become more provisional and tentative.

For you to go forward from here, it's not that you need to find your faith again as much as you need to work through your faith issues. You need to get a handle on your questions and doubts, not by suppressing them but by thinking and praying through them until you return to a place of confidence in God once again. Anything short of this will take you out of step with the Spirit.

One way forward, according to 17th-century philosopher Blaise Pascal, which we find in his posthumously published *Pensées,* is to "wager" on God. No one can satisfactorily (rationally) prove the existence of God, but we can place our bets, so to speak, just as we do in so many relationships, ventures, and groups where we could never prove (ahead of time) whether it is what we hope for or expect. When it comes to faith in God, Pascal argued, if you wager on God, and you're right, you have everything to gain. If you're wrong, you have nothing to lose. If, on the other hand, you wager against God, and you're right, you have gained little or nothing. If you are wrong, you have everything to lose.[2]

Personally, what's most helped me to work through so many of my faith issues has been to actively wrestle with my doubt, fears, disappointments, and longings in conversation with God. As I've struggled with unanswerable questions about the existence of God and the reality of God's presence in my life, my intellect has led me to realize that I cannot settle questions about God intellectually. However, through prayer, personal reflection, and weighing the options before me (whether to believe, what to believe, how to live, and so forth), I find myself being taken back to God and faith over and over again.

I realize, of course, that I cannot prove that God's help is a fact, but I can say that it is a fact that living by faith has improved the quality of my life. Faith in God's love has been the single greatest source of encouragement for me, helping me to accept and forgive myself and to want to be more loving toward others. Faith in God's goodness helps me to get outside of myself, to want to be an agent for good in the world, to seek to be a better person, and to not get stuck in the hole of disillusionment and despair. Faith helps me through times of insecurity, loss, fear, or uncertainty by giving me a rock to stand on, and prayer takes me into God's presence where I often find peace, comfort, joy, strength, and courage in the midst of my

2. See, Pascal, *Pensées*, paragraph 418 (Section 2, Series II).

greatest challenges. And when I can't sense God's presence, or I don't see if or how God is helping, I continue to trust, because what I have in the love, goodness, and working of God cannot be matched by any competing philosophy or secular worldview.

Jesus himself may have died with unanswered questions ("Why have you forsaken me?"), yet he refused to give up his faith. He was mocked for his faith in God the Father, and his detractors pointed to his crucifixion and inability to come down off the cross as proof that he was deluded, out of touch with reality. Yet, even in his death, when God appeared to have forsaken him, Jesus still cried out, "*My* God, *my* God . . . " (Mark 15:34, italics added). Though he did not seem to understand why God was not saving him from death, he still clung to his relationship with God, *his* God, his *abba* Father, until the end.[3] Further, scholars have long noted that Jesus' choice of words come from Psalm 22, which begins with this cry of confusion over his abandonment (22:1) but nonetheless finishes with a triumphant statement of faith concerning the one who felt abandoned by God:

> To him, indeed, shall all who sleep in the earth bow down; before him shall bow all who go down to the dust, and I shall live for him. Posterity will serve him; future generations will be told about the LORD, and proclaim his deliverance to a people yet unborn, saying that he has done it. (Ps 22:29–31, NRSV)

Eventually, we see in Jesus' resurrection that God had not, in fact, abandoned him after all. His faith and faithfulness were vindicated. God's help was real. It came in God's timing in ways that served God's purposes, but God was faithful to him. And that's what Jesus was betting on. That's who Jesus was trusting in.

Faith and disbelief: Two perspectives. Two radically different worldviews. True wisdom is knowing on which to place your wager. For the mature Christian, wisdom also means not abandoning the faith that has been so meaningful and helpful in our lives when our suffering, distress, or anger over the injustice and horrors of this world suddenly cause us to question God and everything we have believed about God and Christ.

---

3. *Abba* is Aramaic for "father." E.g., see Mark 14:36.

But do you really need God?

In 2009, Hollywood produced its own critical take on religion and the human impulse to put their faith in God in the movie *The Answer Man*. The main character, Arlen Faber is a national sensation—a much sought after religions guru, who captured 10 percent of the "Godmarket" after publishing his best-selling book, *God and Me*.

Turns out, though, that his claim to have heard from God is a lie. In fact, he is actually a disillusioned, cynical, dishonest narcissist. Faber sells religion to make money, but doesn't believe his own teaching, and certainly doesn't live by it. As one disappointed fan of *God and Me*—and former fan of Faber—remarks at one point in the story, "He may have written the book, but he sure didn't read it!"

From the screenwriter's disillusionment comes a perspective on religion and life that says, in effect: "Everyone suffers in life, and God—if there is one—won't help. No one truly hears from God, so don't expect answers to your prayers, and certainly don't listen to those who claim to know anything about God. Instead, listen to your heart, and believe in what you can do on your own."

Such an angry rejection of faith and a brave, romantic reliance on human potential may seem understandable and even be inspiring to some, but remains unsatisfying and inadequate for me. The assumptions of secular humanists are naïve and their hope illusory. They may be right to be skeptical of any religious system, but too quick to reject belief in God. They arrogantly take faith in their own abilities, and too easily shortchange the value of seeking a meaningful relationship with God. Ultimately, such faith in self is based on a lie, because it simply cannot deliver on its promise of relieving angst and creating a better world in any lasting, far-reaching way.

So, what's the alternative? Taking God out of the equation certainly isn't the answer for most of us. Rather, for many of us, the solution is to let God transform our hearts and minds by divine love and grace, to look to Christ as the revelation of God and redeemer of humanity, and to let our lives and work flow from the leading of the Holy Spirit. The transformed world that so many long for will never come from secular humanism, a religious system, or any abstract ideology, but only from Christ-centered, Spirit-led human beings who are committed to know, love, and serve a personal God with all their heart, mind, and strength.

We must believe that we are beloved creations of a good Creator, who has provided a Savior to meet our deepest needs, which we cannot meet on our own. Then, as we move from faith to experience, the more we know the love and grace of God for ourselves, the more we will acquire the needed capacity to show that same love and grace to others as well.

Such a vision for life helps us to get beyond our own self-centered clinging to God for our own benefit in order to join God wherever the Spirit is at work doing good. Without such a vision, most of our noble intentions and humanistic ideals for society are going to collapse rather quickly when we don't get what we want or need. Without this kind of personal relationship with God, we simply are not going to have enough to draw on within ourselves to sustain our good intentions.

As we continue to mature, no matter how smart, capable, dedicated, or "lucky" we may be, we still need God. We need God's Spirit to cultivate a heart of love within us. We need Christ to show us how to move beyond selfishness to true devotion to the well-being of others (including those we already love the most). And we need the Holy Spirit to lead us, to guide us, and to empower us to use our abilities, opportunities, and resources in ways that best fit with God's good purposes.

Seeking to know, love, and serve God is not about using belief in God as a crutch when we should be learning how to rely on ourselves more, as if they were mutually exclusive options. Rather, maximizing human potential calls for doing all we can to grow personally and to develop our self-confidence in the context of seeking the kind of relationship with God that will be truly life-giving and service-empowering.

We don't have to choose between faith in God and developing ourselves and creatively and energetically addressing problems and challenges. We just need wisdom to know what part God plays, and what part we play, and how God and we can best work together to do what we simply cannot and never will be able to do on our own.

What if God let you down?

"I volunteered to read to terminally ill children at a cancer unit once, and found that many of them were bound up at first in the hope that God would heal them. He never did. I wept copious tears each time one passed away during my stint, as I had become emotionally attached to them. The pain got to me. And He claimed to have this special caring for children? But why are we blaming him, when he is only imaginary?" (Kadene, 6/7/10)[4]

My heart breaks when I read experiences like these. Sincere people have been deeply hurt or disappointed by God, or they have trusted in others who represent God, and they got a raw deal. They believe that God abandoned them or seriously let them down, just when they most needed God's help.

I understand all of these feelings and reactions very well. I've had them myself. I am convinced that I will never be able to fully understand why God seems to be very helpful in some circumstances, but does nothing in others, especially when a little help could make all the difference in the world to someone who is suffering.

For example, one of the most troubling, difficult, and faith-testing experiences of my life was when my mother was dying slowly of Alzheimer's disease. For nearly fifteen horrible years, I had to watch her suffer and then turn into a mere shell of the person I had loved so much. At first, I prayed that she would be healed, but she wasn't. Then I prayed that God would put her out of her misery (and us out of ours), but she continued to linger on and on. I asked God to spare my father from deteriorating physically while he was trying to care for her, but he went downhill rather quickly and wound up dying four years ahead of Mom.

She was a strong Christian who helped many different people, and she and I were very close. Her death was going to be a huge loss to me. It all seemed so tragic. Why would God let this happen to her? Even though I should have known better, and should have asked this question on behalf of millions of others who suffer far worse horrors, I was caught off guard. I had falsely assumed that if someone was a good person or did good in the world (or was my mother), then God would spare him or her from extraordinary suffering and premature death. But there she was, slowly dying before my eyes. What was I supposed to think now? What was I going to do?

One day, in the midst of my angst and distress, I came to a crossroads. I had become bitter, and I was going to have choose which way I was going to go: continue in my bitterness, choose to trust God in the midst of unanswered questions, or quit believing in God all together. When the options finally crystallized in my mind, I suddenly saw the way forward for me.

4. See Geoffrion, "When Prayer Makes a Difference," to read the article that prompted these responses from bloggers.

To cling to bitterness seemed just plain stupid and self-defeating. Holding a grudge against God and stewing in negative emotions was getting me nowhere and was poisoning my soul. Logically, I had to consider the possibility that God didn't exist or didn't care. However, I had a problem with this option: my belief in God went to the core of my being, and my relationship with God had led to significant changes, meaning, and fruitfulness in my life and relationships, in spite of all of the disappointments and frustrations. Further, the existence and work of a divine being remains the most compelling explanation to me for the universe, the many wonders of life, and human existence.[5]

That left the middle option—humbly accepting that I am not capable of fully understanding God, trusting that God does love me and is active in my life for good, and seeking whatever God offers to me on God's terms.[6] I could leave open unanswerable intellectual questions and focus instead on my experience with Christ and the Holy Spirit, as interpreted in the New Testament. Above all, what I have experienced through the love and grace of God has been the most powerful, life-changing force in my life, which I wouldn't trade for anything.[7]

5. In response to arguments that human suffering is a sign that God does not exist or doesn't care, a number of prominent twentieth- (and now twenty-first) century theologians have suggested in various ways that God may be "powerless" to help in some circumstances, because that is how God set up the world. For example, perhaps God is self-limiting to preserve human freedom, or that there are other constraints due the nature of things. I wasn't well acquainted with this theological perspective when my mother's health was deteriorating. Thinking now that God truly does care about my suffering but that God's hands are "tied," so to speak, for reasons I cannot fully grasp, and that God suffers with humanity as a victim of evil in Jesus' crucifixion and with us as we suffer, does make me feel some better. It's easier to relate to a caring, but helpless, God than to an apathetic or even cruel one. Nevertheless, I am still left with my pain and unanswered questions about why evil exists at all and why God could not have devised a less painful way for humans to learn and grow, even if I do find some comfort in the notion that God is right here suffering along with me. This is not the place to delve any further into the theodicy question, though the ways God can be and is available to us does affect our expectations of God. What we think God is capable of definitely will affect what we trust God for on a day to day basis.

6. The middle option acknowledges that there remain complex theological questions that cannot be satisfactorily answered, an observation that does not invalidate faith but simply acknowledges human limitations and that Scripture doesn't fully address every intellectual question we may have. In choosing this option, I have chosen to focus on what is accessible to me through faith in Christ and my experience with the Holy Spirit.

7. See *The Spirit-Led Leader*, 193–95, and Chapter 8, footnote 10, above.

In that moment, I suddenly knew what choice I was going to make. Or perhaps I should say, it was made for me. I was given the grace to trust again in God. I accepted that I would wrestle with important questions about God, but that they need not hold me back from living by faith and enjoying a relationship with God.[8]

When the light came on, I suddenly was set free from the bitterness I felt and free to love and serve God again wholeheartedly. You might even say, I forgave God in that moment. Not that God needed forgiving, but in my own small mind, arrogant enough to think that I should be able to understand God and all of God's ways, I needed to let go of my charges against God.

That's what forgiveness is. Letting go of real or imagined offenses and choosing to go on with the relationship on a new basis—sometimes with renewed hope, and sometimes with altered expectations. Either way, humbling ourselves, forgiving God, and embracing what is available to us through Christ, is often the way to a fresh start in our relationships with God.

Keeping in step with the Spirit calls for going to God—not avoiding or running away from God—with our deepest pain and unanswered questions. Each of us has to work through our doubts and struggles individually until we get to the place where we can once again wholeheartedly offer our "yes" to God and trust enough to go forward all in.

When others let you down

Sometimes, through prayer and perseverance, things have a way of working out. And sometimes they don't.

Think for a moment about those times when you tried to serve Christ, to step out in faith, to step outside of your comfort zone to reach out to someone or do something good in the world, and it flopped. Maybe you were burned. You were duped or totally misread the situation and got sucked into something that wasn't what you thought, and the outcome was far from what you expected or wanted. Maybe you were just disappointed by the other person(s), the project, the results, or simply the experience itself.

8. In *The Spirit-Led Leader*, 175–78, I tell the same story I do here, only there I do so to illustrate how trust in God is a choice, not the logical outcome of a fact-based, analytical process that claims to prove God's trustworthiness.

And now you're unhappy. You didn't like what happened. Maybe you've stepped back as a result. You're not sure what to think, and you're not sure what you're going to do now. You may have firmly believed the Holy Spirit led you to get involved, and now you're wondering if you and God had a misunderstanding. Or worse, perhaps you suspect that you fooled yourself when you thought the Holy Spirit was prompting you, and now you're not sure what or whom to trust.

What does Spirit-led living look like going forward from here?

When you're not sure what to think

It's not uncommon in Christian ministry or when trying to help someone in need, to end up a little (or a lot) disillusioned. For me personally, there have been many times when I felt taken advantage of and became resentful. More frequently than I'd like to admit, I'm just disappointed. No one deceived me. Others did what they said they would. But the end result didn't produce the feeling in me I was hoping for. Perhaps the individual or organization I was helping didn't live up to my expectations, or didn't show appreciation in the ways I was looking for. Perhaps I assumed I would feel more satisfaction or joy, but I walked away feeling empty.

Not uncommonly, I have felt a little confused or even angry, especially when others disappoint me or the experience troubles me for some reason. I wonder, is this what I should expect from trying to help others? From Christian community? From trying to bridge the gap between haves and have nots? At such times, I want to learn from the experience. I want to become wiser and less naïve; but I don't want to become so cynical that I find a convenient excuse to turn back, to stop following my heart, to reinterpret the voice of the Spirit in any way that clamps down on the mission of love.

After all, Jesus was crucified by some of the people he tried to minister to. Why should I think that ministry and doing good in the world will always, or even often, end up like a fairy tale with happy endings and happy feelings all around? Or, as one wise pastor told another pastor who was complaining about how he was being treated by parishioners, "What makes you think that you should suffer less than your Lord?"

Still, what are we to think from such disappointing, disillusioning, and sometimes embarrassing, humiliating, or infuriating experiences? What does it mean to keep the faith as a Spirit-led follower of Christ?

What my dad taught me
about disillusionment

Dad was not a philosopher or much of a theologian. Like most of us, he could not explain why innocent people suffer or why his mother and father had to suffer as they did, why he and his wife had to suffer as they had, or why some people believe in God and some people don't.

But Dad wasn't fazed by what he didn't know or couldn't do. He believed there is a God who loves us and became a human being in Jesus to prove that love to us. He believed he needed God's forgiveness and God's salvation along with the rest of humanity. Dad struggled and suffered much, but also felt he was helped and blessed much. He was sometimes confused about why God does things the way God does, but he still put his trust in the God of the Bible and the Jesus of history.

His life and feelings were a bit like those we find in the biblical book of Lamentations. After a lot of suffering and heartache, the writer says,

> I remember my affliction and my wandering,
> the bitterness and the gall.
> I well remember them,
> and my soul is downcast within me.
> Yet this I call to mind
> and therefore I have hope:
> Because of the LORD's great love we are not consumed
> for his compassions never fail.
> They are new every morning;
> Great is your faithfulness.
> I say to myself, "The LORD is my portion;
> therefore I will wait for him."
> (Lam 3: 19–24)

Dad did a lot of "waiting" in his lifetime, especially in the last decades of his life. And in some respects, he died "waiting" for God to act on his behalf. You might say, he died "disillusioned," in the best sense of the word. Not without faith, but without the illusion that God would heal all his illnesses, deliver his wife from Alzheimer's disease, or rescue them in some other way in this life.

If you feel disappointed or let down by God you may be in the process of being dis-illusioned. That is, your illusions about life and/or God are being stripped away from you. Like a band-aid being ripped off tender skin, it hurts a lot, but some time that band-aid has to come off . . . and so do your illusions that somehow you deserve a break in life, or that God is going to make everything better, or that you should be spared from the suffering others have to face for whatever reason you have conjured up to deny the reality about life.

Life is difficult. Life is unfair and sometimes brutal. Life ends in death for everyone. As the famous psychiatrist Scott Peck so eloquently described to us decades ago in *The Road Less Traveled*, it is those who accept this truth who are best prepared to live the life that is available for us. When we realize that suffering is part of life that we cannot avoid and will not be rescued from, our dis-illusionment can be the first step toward actually facing reality constructively.

So disillusionment can be a friend, if we do not get stuck in anger, bitterness or self-absorption. It helps us to face the truth about real life and forces us to ask important questions like, "What can I believe about God that will hold up in my experience?" "What can I look to God for?" "What is the meaning of a real relationship with God?" Disillusionment can be the first step toward looking to God for what God truly has to offer: a sense of meaning, purpose, and hope that can exist in the midst of suffering and loss, precisely because God points us to what extends beyond the suffering and loss. When we let go of needing God to fix our current problem or spare us from pain, we become more open to the Spirit's comforting presence. We may start looking for the meaning of life in our relationship with God and in the sacred love flow rather than in pursuing the American dream, materialism, success, fame, pleasure, or any other inferior rival. We will pray for an ability to serve God's purposes in the midst of our suffering—such as by focusing on the needs of others, who observe us or look to us as models of faith, hope, and love.

When I held my dad's hand in his final days, or steadied him as he tried in vain to walk, or gently kissed him on the forehead good night, I knew I was losing a great friend, but what he gave me was not being lost. And when I cried out to God for some kind of understanding or explanation, my only comfort was believing that this life (and death in it) is not all that there is. There is something more. There is hope.

No one can answer all the questions we have or prove God's existence or love. The evidence is ambiguous at best. In the end, faith is just that, faith. It is "being sure of what we hope for and certain of what we do not see" (Heb 11:1). For those who have it, there is a peace and a hope that helps them face suffering and death. That is what Dad clung to in his darkest hours, and that is what he wanted for his sons, his family, and his friends more than anything else.

In order to be able to flow with the Spirit, we must hold on to our faith that God is indeed reaching out to us, and that God can be trusted. This holds for ourselves, and also for what we think about God's relationship with others.

Your next Spirit-led steps

Are you struggling to keep your faith? Perhaps it is your suffering, the pain of others, frustration with trying to love someone, disappointment with God or those you trusted, or troubling questions that are upsetting you. If so, make a list of those people and situations. Reflect on the questions raised for you and the effect those unanswered questions are having on your faith, motivation, and faithfulness.

Without suppressing your questions or denying your feelings, what would "keeping the faith" look like for you? What difference would it make if you chose to trust in God in the midst of your unanswered questions? Write down your thoughts in your spiritual journal. Share your feelings and questions with God in prayer, and with a trusted friend or mentor.

On the chance that you are one of those who identify with the angry readers of my Huffington Post blog, and you're still reading this late into the chapter, I don't know what kind of raw deal you might have experienced in your life, or what impact it might be having on your relationship with God. You may feel you have a right to be angry at God, and really good reason to reject religion or faith in God. You probably do. But if you are turning your back on God and prayer, what do you have now that you didn't have when you put your trust in God? What have you lost by distancing yourself from God?

What would happen if you chose to forgive God for not helping you when you expected or begged for help? What might happen if you chose to move toward God, instead of away from God, with all of your hurt and pain? I know you might instinctively respond, "Nothing! Nothing would happen!" However, that is not my experience. You may not experience what you want or expect, but, in time, those who put their hope in God will likely know and experience the Father's love and presence once again.

11

Ask for the Help You Need

Let us then approach the throne of grace with confidence,
so that we may receive mercy and find grace to help us
in our time of need.

HEBREWS 4:16

WHEN OTHERS COME TO you for guidance or for answers for their lives, what do they tend to be looking for? What do they most need from you? When you're the one who needs help on your spiritual journey, what do you usually need? How comfortable are you asking for it?

Among those who seek spiritual counsel or coaching from me, all of them have at least one thing in common. They all want help and are willing to ask for it. They all want to serve Christ, but often they're not sure how the Spirit is leading or how to pursue their vision or dream. Or, if they know, they need help in strategizing or working through or around the "walls" that have been holding them back. Some are in a discernment process and know that they need others to be listening with them or to help them think through the relevant issues. Others want help finding some fresh solutions to old problems, or simply to hold them accountable to the commitments they make.

"Paul," for example, was very successful running a family business but he didn't know how to develop a stronger relationship with God or how to create a better marriage. "Ted" had made millions of dollars in finance but was jealous of the peace his wife felt when she went through a life-threatening illness. Could I help him find that kind of peace and learn what it means to be Spirit-led? "Jerry" loved his relationship with God but felt utterly frustrated in his desire to go to the next level of leadership. Could I help him listen to God to get some answers? As it turned out, he really had no idea what kind of help he needed, but the critical point is, he knew he needed something and was open to looking for it.

"Pam" felt that God was calling her to a new chapter in her ministry. She was certain of her feelings and excited about an opportunity that was emerging, but she didn't feel confident at all that she could discern the Spirit's leading on her own. "Betty" had a dream of opening a shelter for unwed mothers, but she was the primary breadwinner for her family. How was she supposed to make sense of the passion she felt, the responsibility that was hers, and the nudging of the Holy Spirit?

"Lloyd" had struggled in vain to quit watching pornography. He loved Christ and served effectively in a leadership role, but when the urge came to surf the adult sites he felt powerless. Given his position, he was reluctant to reveal his secret; yet, in the end, he took the risk to open up because he knew he needed help. "Susan" was highly respected and effective in her role as a teacher, but she felt so much guilt and shame from secrets in her life. She had asked for forgiveness so many times, but still felt ashamed and like a fraud. What could help her to find forgiveness and peace from the past and confidence to still use her gifts in leadership?

Many times, coaching clients want me to solve their problems or provide the answers they're looking for. One successful salesman, "Randy," once threw up his hands after several hard sessions and said with exasperation, "I just want you to tell me what to do!" We both laughed. I explained what I almost always have to explain to those who come to me for guidance: "I am here to help you, but not to give you the answers." And why? Because the help we most need from a coach, pastor, spiritual advisor, or trusted friend is not to do our thinking or listening to God for us, but to teach us how to listen better to the Spirit for ourselves.

Asking for help is healthy and wise, but the kind of help one seeks and how the help is offered are also very important. Seeking help from others should complement, rather than replace, our own efforts. The help we need is not to short-circuit our own struggle to grow personally and spiritually. As followers of Christ we need to keep growing in our ability to listen to and to cooperate with the Spirit for ourselves so that we can make proper use of the counsel and support of others who are listening, praying, and seeking guidance from God with us. Keeping in step with the Spirit requires striking a balance between taking personal responsibility for one's life and relationship with God and seeking the right kind of input and help from one's community, whether it is submitting to elders and authority figures or getting counsel from trusted friends, pastors, and advisors.

Start with God

Practically, whether we are seeking help to know what to do, how to do it, or for a greater ability to do it, the place to start is in prayer. Listening for the voice of God continues to be the fundamental component for one's spiritual life. As we seek God's guidance, we should fully expect that the Spirit will send us out into the world to receive help from others and to learn more from the Spirit in the process of acting in faith and serving. But the place to begin is on our knees. There, in humility and openness, we ask God to show us what we most need and to guide us in a process of seeing and doing all that is necessary to think straight, to stay in the sacred love flow, and to fulfill God's purposes for our lives.

All of us at times need the Holy Spirit to open our eyes to something that we've not been able to see, but need to, in order to cope with some situation at hand and move forward. We also need the Holy Spirit to work in us or in whomever else may be involved in our lives in order to shift something internally so that God's love and power will be able to flow more freely. By all means, if we already know what we need to do, then we should just do it. But, in my experience, often I feel like I just can't make the needed changes on my own; and I certainly can't produce any desired changes in someone else. Prayer is asking God both to help us see what we can and need to do, and it's asking for God to do in us, in others, and in the situation in general what we cannot do.

For example, perhaps you've been working hard and putting yourself out to try to help a group of people, but their response is disappointing. You're feeling more and more frustrated or discouraged. You want a different outcome, but you just can't figure out what's wrong or what to do differently. Maybe you're getting angry, and you feel like lashing out. Perhaps you feel like giving up all together.

When I get in these kinds of situation, my first instinct is often reactive. I vacillate between going on the attack and wanting to quit (fight or flight). Or, as psychologists have observed, a third response to danger or distress is to freeze up in the face of a threat. I can do that, too. Clamming up when a verbal response is called for or not doing anything when something truly needs to be done. I know that these are not constructive responses, but it seems nearly impossible to respond otherwise at times. So, I ask for God's help.

Reaching out to the Holy Spirit in such circumstances may simply be a quick, desperate plea, asking for God to solve the problem for us. But when we have sufficient emotional strength and mental space, our prayers can go deeper. We can ask for more insight into ourselves, into what we're thinking or doing that is contributing to the problem. We can ask for eyes to see the other person more clearly or to see what is happening in the dynamics of the relationship or group that might help us to understand, to empathize, and to respond more compassionately, wisely, and lovingly. We may also need eyes to see when someone else is not being honest, reasonable, or faithful, so that we can respond less naively and take a stand to protect ourselves or others.

And when everything inside of us is screaming and objecting to how the Spirit seems to be leading, we can work that out, too, in the context of prayer.

When I was at my wit's end

One particular event immediately comes to mind when I really was at my wit's end. I was leading a week-long spiritual retreat in the Chartres Cathedral in France. Everything I tried was met with resistance. I was frustrated, angry, and felt like giving up. I had to face the fact that my current approach to teaching my sessions was not working, and was not going to work. I had to try to see the situation through the eyes of my participants who were annoying me, and imagine what they might be feeling and needing. I had to stop blaming others for the disappointing and frustrating situation, and start thinking creatively. I had a choice to make. Would I stay stuck in my current feelings and just press through anyway? Or, would I step back to get a fresh perspective, be open to change, and ask the Holy Spirit to show me the way?

Fortunately, by the grace of God, I chose the latter approach during that retreat. But this choice did not come without a fight. Within me, that is. I had to die to the teaching I wanted to give, and then I had to allow new ideas and different methods to surface. Specifically, in retrospect I realize that I had to do at least ten things to make the shift.

1. I needed to take some time to be by myself and to avoid the temptation to take out my frustration on class members.

2. I went for a long prayer walk. In this case, I had the opportunity to walk the labyrinth inside the Chartres Cathedral three times, surrounded by images of Jesus and other biblical characters.

3. I let off steam by muttering under my breath and by making faces for my wife's camera.

4. I consciously let myself feel all of my feelings (frustration, disappointment, hurt, anger). I didn't feed them, but neither did I try to talk myself out of them. I let the feelings surge within me. I named them, without judging them. At first they grew stronger, and then, before long, they started to lose their power and began to dissipate.

5. I spent a long time journaling to get my thoughts and feelings out on paper so that I could see what was going on inside me, and so that I could observe myself from a little distance, and assess better what was truly going on.

6. Through all of this, and probably most importantly, I was praying. First complaining to God, then asking for help: What do I need to see here? What do I need to let go of? What can I do differently? What do these retreatants most need, and what do they most need from me?

7. I contemplated *Le Beau Dieu* (The Beautiful God), a statue of Jesus on the south porch of the cathedral. As I stood there just looking at the figure, I asked Jesus (not the statue) what he would do. Almost immediately my eyes fell to the Bible the Jesus figure was holding. The message seemed clear: "Get back to letting the class sessions flow directly out of Scripture."

8. I sat down and rethought the next teaching session from the beginning, based on the language, approach, and content that the class members would find most helpful, instead of what I most wanted to teach them.

9. I went out to dinner with friends to stop obsessing on the experience, but then got up at 5:30 AM the next morning to spend extra time thinking and praying before rejoining the rest of the group.

10. Though the pilgrims I was leading had not done anything wrong, I forgave them for not being the way I wanted them to be. (What I was

actually doing was choosing to accept them and stop blaming them for my frustration and theirs.) I needed to clear away the negative feelings that grew out of my reaction to them. I forgave myself for missing the mark with my teaching and not figuring out what they needed faster.

To my surprise and delight, the new attitude, new material, and new approach made a huge difference. Between my willingness to change, whatever spiritual work they had done unbeknownst to me, and the moving of the Holy Spirit, the teaching time flowed powerfully once again.

I still wish I could have taught what I wanted to teach, in the way I wanted to do it; but something else was needed in this context, with these particular individuals, at this unique time in their lives. On my own I might have just kept trying the failed approach hoping for a different result; but by reaching out to the Holy Spirit for help in numerous ways, I came to see what I had not be able to see before. I took responsibility to address the problem directly and to seek out the help I needed, but it was the Spirit who helped create a shift in my attitude and heart that breathed new life into me and into my interaction with the group.

When the help we need is encouragement[1]

Sometimes the help that we need from God is mostly encouragement. We need to know that God has not abandoned us, still loves us, and can comfort us in the midst of our struggle and suffering. We long for a touch of the presence of God to give us hope and an ability to face our troubles without being swallowed up or even destroyed by them.

Almost everyone we meet in countries where there has been a lot of oppression and suffering looks back at us through tired eyes. They wear their weariness in their posture. Their faces are often creased with lines etched by fear and anxiety—be they from years of tribulation or a single night of horror. Children and violated women sometimes just stare with hollow expressions, emptied of life by unspeakable atrocities witnessed or experienced personally. Even the most hopeful and motivated individuals have trouble masking their quiet despair and resignation to overwhelming forces beyond their control.

---

1. Portions of this section are excerpted from my Huffington Post post, "When Prayer Makes a Difference in Suffering."

In such circumstances, where so many suffer from poverty, war, op-pression, hunger, disease, and sexual violence, what's needed is something far deeper than just theories and practices that work well in safe environ-ments with ample resources. Consistently, in our work in developing coun-tries, we meet students, community leaders, and pastors who are clinging closely to God in the midst of seemingly overwhelming problems and pain. They tell us that through prayer, they find peace and strength that they cannot access otherwise.

When we go to prayer to ask for whatever help we need, we are right to pray for any and everything on our heart. Yet, what I've learned from my brothers and sisters in Christ who must cope with sometimes unimaginable suffering and deprivation is that just praying itself is helpful. Just taking the concerns to God, and releasing anxiety and worry, is in itself a great help and source of comfort.

As I mentioned in chapter 9, the Apostle Paul described the peace-producing prayer process this way when he instructed the Philippians, "Do not be anxious about anything, but in everything, by prayer and petition, with thanksgiving, present your requests to God. And the peace of God, which transcends all understanding, will guard your hearts and your minds in Christ Jesus" (Phil 4:6–7). Many of us know or assume we are going to continue to suffer, but we pray so that we can experience God's comforting presence in the midst of our suffering.

What the psalmist says about asking for help

The psalmists knew very well what it is like to plea for help in the midst of distressing or menacing circumstances. When the threat to them was physi-cal, they would, not surprisingly, frequently pray for confusion for the enemy and victory for Israel, either as personal vindication or actual military suc-cess. Sometimes, they prayed for the nation and sometimes for themselves personally in the midst of the threatening circumstances. But of greatest im-portance is their realization that sometimes their last, best, and greatest hope was simply the LORD. That is, they found through their personal experience with God what they needed to stand strong and carry on.

Take Psalm 94 as just one example. The psalmist writes:

> Who will rise up for me against the wicked?
> Who will take a stand for me against evildoers?
> Unless the LORD had given me help,
> I would soon have dwelt in the silence of death.
> When I said, "My foot is slipping,"
> your love, O LORD, supported me. (Psalm 94:16–18)

On the surface, these verses appear to be a typical call for help to overcome the psalmist's enemies. Indeed, in context, defeating the enemies of the LORD and the king is precisely what the writer seemed to have in mind. However, there is more being expressed in these verses. First of all, verses 17 and 18 function as a chiasmus, a common Hebrew literary device by which the same idea is presented in successive verses, but in reverse order. By identifying this form, we gain greater understanding into the psalmist's thinking and faith. In this case, we can identify the following ABBA pattern:

A Unless the LORD had given me help,

   B I would soon have dwelt in the silence of death.

   B When I said, "My foot is slipping,"

A your love, O LORD, supported me.

By recognizing the chiasmic pattern, we can see that psalmist's reference to his foot slipping (B) meant that he feared he would die (B). The support the LORD gave him was not, or not only, as one would expect, i.e., deliverance from his enemy. The help the LORD gave him (A) was love or loving-kindness (A).[2] In other words, from an experience of the love of the LORD, the psalmist felt supported, and his foot was kept from slipping (i.e., his fear of death did not overwhelm him).

This psychological and spiritual interpretation of these verses is supported not only by the chiastic structure of verses 17–18, but where the psalmist goes next in verse 19, which stands in parallel to verse 18.[3] He adds, "When anxiety was great within me, your consolation brought joy to my soul" (94:19). Hebrew parallelism in its simplest form presents an ABAB pattern as follows.

2. The Hebrew, *chesed*, may be translated as "love" or "loving-kindness." Here, in Psalm 94:18, the NIV translates *chesed* as "love"; the NRSV, "steadfast love"; and the NASB, "loving-kindness."

3. Hebrew parallelism is another rhetorical literary device, which highlights an important idea by repeating it in different language.

A When I said, "My foot is slipping,"

    B your love, O LORD, supported me.

A When anxiety was great within me,

    B your consolation brought joy to my soul.

What we learn from this observation is that the psalmist's experience of his foot slipping (A) was an anxious experience (A, not just a threat of physical danger). The experience of the LORD's love (B) was a consolation (perhaps assurance or confidence for the future, not necessarily deliverance in the past) that brought him joy (B).

In our suffering, or when faced with overwhelming challenges or threatening circumstances, sometimes we reach a point where all we can do is pray. Perhaps the situation is so overwhelming, so painful or utterly bleak that we've given up hope. We may even feel as the psalmist did, that our foot is slipping, and we may soon succumb to despair or even death itself. Yet, it is in prayer, that we find the support we need to not fall. What provides such strength? It is not from the hoped for victory or deliverance (though that would help immensely). Rather our strength and comfort in the midst of our suffering and difficulties comes from the loving-kindness of the LORD.

Conclusion

None of us is capable of fulfilling the will of God on our own. We need the help of Christ and the Holy Spirit. We need the help of our brothers and sisters in Christ. We need the help of a wide range of people and resources that God can use to shape our thinking, strengthen our capabilities, and encourage us to press forward when we've lost heart or gotten out of step with the Spirit for whatever reason.

At the beginning of this chapter, we looked at numerous examples of the kinds of help individuals are looking for when they become serious about growing spiritually and keeping in step with the Spirit. Many of them learned that the help they needed was not just answers to their questions from some spiritual guru or authority figure. Rather, they needed to grow in their own relationship with God so that they could learn how to listen better for the leading of the Spirit for themselves. Without exception, those who were willing to admit their need for help and were open to listening to God experienced the Holy Spirit speaking within their hearts or minds, either during a prayer session or through coaching.

Asking for help doesn't stop with prayer, of course, but continues through a process of listening to the Spirit on an ongoing basis and by taking action in response to the leading received. For example, at the end of every coaching session, each person identifies very specific action steps to take in the coming week that naturally grow out of our time of praying and talking together. Nothing is forced. It all flows comfortably, even if the action step is a little scary or foreign.

Do this. Do that. Journal on this. Reflect on that. Contact him. Ask her. Make out a plan. Work the plan. Practice a spiritual discipline. Step back. Step forward. Each situation is unique. Each set of action steps is different from week to week, person to person. The point is, in order to keep in step with the Spirit, we have to listen to God, ask for the help we need, and take action to put our "yes" into motion as soon as we're ready to do so.

If emotionally we're not ready to go forward, then our best action step may actually be to step back. We may need to disengage from our emotional reactions to whatever we're dealing with, step back far enough to get perspective, and look at the big picture. What is going on? What is the right perspective on the situation? What is our heart or mind or body telling us? What is holding us back? How would we advise someone else who is in our situation?

As we talked about in chapter 8, when our inability to keep in step with the Spirit is sin, the help we need is repentance, and the Spirit can help us get there if we cannot repent on our own. Likewise, with addictions and other deeply ingrained habits and patterns of destructive thinking and behavior, the help we need will almost certainly involve others, such as pastors, professional counselors, therapy, recovery groups, and accountability partners.

When we try to fulfill our callings on our own, we bolster our self-confidence by saying things to ourselves like "I can do this!" Motivational, perhaps, but such a rally cry can easily throw us back on our egos, which may help us to accomplish the task at hand but may also sow the seeds for pride and self-reliance, which ultimately cannot take us all the way to where God is calling us. When we go to the other extreme and face our weaknesses, sinfulness, and powerlessness, we admit, "I cannot do this. I cannot be the person God is calling me to be." Truthful and necessary for spiritual growth, for certain, but if we stay at this point we may become demoralized and give up altogether. A third option comes from the Apostle Paul, who said, "I can do all things through him [Christ] who gives me strength" (Phil 4:13). In context, Paul was communicating to the Philippians that, on his own, he might not be able to handle the trials and temptations that he had to face in his life—whether it was imprisonment, lack of food, or threat of death, on one extreme; or religious achievement, high status, or abundance, on the other. Paul models humble, but strong self-confidence that is rooted in unshakable God-confidence.

No matter what we may be struggling with, keeping in step with the Spirit calls for humbly putting ourselves in a posture of prayer to listen for the voice of God, remaining open to whatever the Spirit may say, and staying ready to take action. From day to day, keeping in step with the Spirit means living in the sacred love flow and doing what we already know to do, with or without a special prompting of the Spirit. When we feel stuck or confused, or find ourselves outside of the flow of the Spirit, it's time to reach out again for whatever help we need. Sometimes we will seek wisdom and guidance, other times support and encouragement. Sometimes it is mercy and grace, other times strength and courage. We must both acknowledge our limitations and simultaneously trust in what God can do in and through us. We must ask for the help we need.

Your next Spirit-led steps

Many of us who are leaders, mentors, caregivers, teachers, pastors, or who function in some other kind of advising role are usually eager to help others, but can be reluctant to admit that sometimes we, the helpers, need help ourselves. Even when we know we need it, sometimes we just can't or won't bring ourselves to reach out for it. But we must learn to do so.

What help do you need right now?

Do you need to listen better, to be more cooperative, to be more humble and open, to think through your options and opportunities, to be more responsive, to make a commitment, or to follow through on a commitment you've already made? Do you need to live more fully in the sacred love flow or to forgive someone? Are you struggling to keep your faith in the midst of suffering and unanswered questions? Are you experiencing the crippling effects of anxiety or confusion? Do you need strength to face the darkest parts of yourself and the darkness you are encountering as you seek to do good in the world?

Wherever you sense a lack or a desire to be more or do more, ask for the help you need. Whatever is holding you up or taking you off track, ask for the help you need. Even when you simply want some encouragement or greater support, ask for the help you need.

Identify your thoughts and feelings that are arising after reading this chapter. Make a list of wherever you are feeling stuck, confused, unsure, discouraged, or some other feeling that is hindering your ability to be led by the Spirit. Make the items as specific as possible. Write down next to each one where you could look for that help, and whom you could ask for the help you need. If you're ready to commit to taking action, indicate when you are going to do it. What, where, and when. And then share your plan with a trusted friend or mentor. If you're not ready, step back and prayerfully ask yourself, why not?

12

Live Your "Yes"

Simply let your 'Yes' be 'Yes,' and your 'No,' 'No';
anything beyond this comes from the evil one.

MATTHEW 5:37

It STARTED IN THE early 2000's when I became increasingly uncomfortable with just being a tourist. I didn't like spending so much time and money on travel without doing a lot more to contribute personally to the many needs in the world. I heard myself say repeatedly, "Enough of just being sight-seers! If we're going to travel so much, I want to do something constructive. I want to teach, serve, or help others in some other way during our weeks abroad."

Burning, existential, spiritual questions

No matter what we did, I couldn't avoid a set of questions that kept bugging me and just had to be answered. I suspect that part of the reason I felt unsure about the answers is that I didn't always want to hear what the Spirit was saying to me. But at the same time, I did want to know. As time went on, I realized that I was never going to be satisfied— or at peace—until I faced whatever the Spirit wanted to say to me.

What was plaguing me the most was the huge discrepancy between my comfortable life in the United States and the massive poverty, distress, and suffering I was seeing around the world. I also saw that we have seminaries throughout the United States and extensive theological libraries to serve an amply resourced US church, while the church in most developing countries is growing at a much faster rate but without adequate training or theological resources for its pastors and leaders.

When I walk the streets of Rwanda and Congo, ride on the back of motorbikes in Vietnam, risk my life in taxis on the streets of Yangon, talk in hushed tones with Christians who suffer persecution or fear for their safety in Central Asia, questions come to mind. I'm not wondering so much about the plight of those who suffer now, but about how the Holy Spirit is leading me to respond to the needs I see. In light of the gross inequities and great suffering for so many throughout the world, and the critical need for leadership development and training . . .

- What does it mean *for me* to be faithful to God?

- What does it mean *for me* to renounce myself and pick up my cross daily to follow Christ?

- What does God truly want *me* to give of myself and my resources?

I wasn't looking for trite answers here. I already knew what the Bible says about each of these questions for followers of Jesus in general. I was trying to pierce the fog of self-deception and cultural blindness to see the truth about how I have been living out my faith (or not) and what was truly in my heart related to my possessions and attachment to my own comfort and security.

I didn't have an axe to grind. I wasn't reacting or eager to tell others what they should do. I wanted the Gospel that I preach to others to continue its revolutionary work in my life in all of the ways that Jesus intended. I wanted to better serve Christ and his church, and not keep tripping so much over my own stubborn, self-centered, self-serving tendencies.

I felt pretty calm when facing these questions, on one hand; and yet was increasingly feeling desperate, on the other. Not desperate so much out of anxiety or fear, but out of a growing sense of the enormous need in the world and my minuscule capacity to do much about it. I wanted to do more, and I wanted to be more. And so, in my growing desperation, I became more and more aware that I had to make some choices—maybe some radical choices—if the future was going to be any different than the past. I'm talking about making changes in how I respond to the prompting of the Holy Spirit in every possible context of my life, and in how I give of myself and my resources to others on a regular basis.

Here's the problem at its core: I want the best of both worlds. I have spent most of my adult life both attempting to enjoy a meaningful relationship with God and to minister effectively to others, while simultaneously trying to please myself on the margins. Increasingly, this kind of mind-set and behavior seemed double-minded to me. Or at least, I wasn't at all satisfied.

I began to see that the appropriate meta-question for my life was not, "How much can I do for Christ and his kingdom, given that I will continue to serve myself as well as possible?" The question has increasingly become, "What could I do—or, better, what would God do through me—if only I would let go of my self-serving choices and behavior in every possible area of my life?" The former question attempts to follow the leading of the Spirit with shackles and weights around my ankles. The latter persistently pursues freedom from "everything that hinders and the sin that so easily entangles" so that I can better "run with perseverance the race marked out for [me]" (Heb 12:1).

Expect the Holy Spirit to work through your questions

The more I kept asking questions like this one and was not be afraid of what the Holy Spirit might show me, the more God helped me to find answers. What the Spirit seems to do is work through a process of raising questions in my consciousness and drawing me to Christ to look for answers.

I ask the same questions over and over, and, in the process, I become more aware of both my resistance to changing and the depth of my desire to change. As I truly open myself to the Spirit and ask for the help I need to hear what I need to hear, and to see what I need to see, greater clarity and conviction emerges. Often little by little, not always with words or concepts, I begin to feel the shifts. I can see that I'm changing for the better.

The real turning point, vocationally, came when I started going to Bulgaria. Three years in a row I spent a week teaching pastors, spouses, and church leaders. I loved the experience of teaching, but at a much deeper level, I felt a sense of satisfaction to be serving very poor Christian leaders who were hungry for teaching and leadership development but did not have access to the same resources so many enjoy in the United States.

On the way home from the third trip to Bulgaria, I wrote my letter of resignation from the ministry I was leading in Minneapolis. The work in Minnesota was close to my heart and it was a privilege to be part of it; but the Spirit was calling me to venture further out of my comfort zone, and had showed me how much he would bless my cooperation. To stay where I was, as good as the ministry was, would have been to say "no" to the Spirit. To stay in the flow of the Spirit, I had to say "yes."

I began traveling to places like Rwanda, Congo, and Myanmar to teach, lead spiritual retreats, build labyrinths for prayer, offer leadership coaching, and serve in whatever ways were most needed in each context—sometimes working with my wife and sometimes working independently. I've loved the ministries, in spite of the sicknesses, the pulmonary embolism that nearly killed my wife, long stretches of time separated from each other and from our sons, and many other difficulties and dangers along the way. I have received so many confirmations that stepping out in faith has been a good thing to do and fits with how God has wanted to use me.

I can see that my choices have been changing, and I am increasingly comfortable with living in uncomfortable settings. I'm more willing and able to manage the stress of extensive travel and lack of certain amenities that I have come to expect back in the States. I rue less the lack of time for friends, play, and pleasures of American life as I dive deeper and deeper into a life of ministry and service, living among the poor, and rubbing shoulders regularly with brothers and sisters in Christ abroad, indigenous to each setting where we serve, whose commitment often seems much greater than mine and who inspire me by their own sacrifice and devotion.

I'm still a bit uncomfortable with this Spirit-led process at times. I mean, asking tough questions and bracing myself for whatever the Spirit might say. I don't feel in control, and I'm a little (a lot?) worried sometimes about where all this might go. At the same time, it feels right. And, the fruit of the leading so far has convinced me that I am on the right track, even if I still make many mistakes, stumble embarrassingly at times, and have so much to learn.

Keep going

Do you know that disturbing, unsettled feeling that I've been talking about? You're feeling a lot of inner turmoil, and you don't know what to think or what it all means. You realize you're getting a signal that something important is happening within you, but you're not sure what to do with the feelings or how to go forward.

Periodically, I go through new spells of uncertainty and agonize over new questions that pit different values against one another, usually a desire to press forward with international work versus practical matters of safety, health, marriage, and family. For example, sometimes I feel great inner tension when I am invited to minister in a country where my wife and I may not be safe. I have to decide if I will accept the call or hold back out of fear. Do I lack faith or am I just being prudent? Volatile financial markets make me wonder, do I pull back to provide better for family or press forward with the ministry with fewer assurances for myself?

After my first couple of trips to serve in Africa, I would return back to Chartres, France (our European home base) feeling all mixed up inside. I felt like I had gotten in way over my head and yet was being called to go even deeper. After one particular trip to Rwanda, we stopped off in Chartres to drop off our "Africa suitcase" for our trip to Congo the following winter. With an aching heart and spinning head, I found my way to the Cathedral to pray. In my distress, I was being drawn to God. I needed comfort, and I wanted help.

I sat awhile in front of Jesus of the Sacred Heart statue, contemplating Jesus' compassion and asking God to alleviate the suffering of the Rwandan Christians. I stayed even longer in the apsidal chapel, contemplating the crucifix. Surely "the Man of Sorrows" had something to say to me that might help. I sat, I watched, I listened.

What was I supposed to learn from everything I saw and experienced? Was God calling me to do something more or differently? If so, what? Many thoughts and ideas raced through my head. However, the most powerful notion was not of any specific heroic act of service. Rather, what I sensed in that quiet place of prayer was simply a call to keep going.

The Holy Spirit was saying, "Take the next step of faith. Don't stop now. Don't be afraid. Don't worry about what I might ask of you. Let all that you are experiencing penetrate your heart as deeply as you can, and let it change you. I am taking you deeper and deeper in our relationship, and I will show you what I want you to do for these people . . . ."

There are countless reasons why any of us may be all mixed up inside. However, the reason we are upset is not as important as what God wants to do in us through our distress. Our turmoil is an opportunity to draw closer to God and to be transformed in some way. At least in principle, Jesus' life and death show us the way forward.

> We know love by this, that [Jesus Christ] laid down his life for us—and we ought to lay down our lives for one another. How does God's love abide in anyone who has the world's goods and sees a

brother or sister in need and yet refuses help? Little children, let us love, not in word or speech, but in truth and action. (1 John 3:16–18, NRSV)

More fully described, this Spirit-led questioning and responding process entails at least four steps that we must take over and over again:

- Listen to the questions that bubble up within you.
- Trust that the Holy Spirit is already in the mix, prompting you, drawing you to Christ, and leading you in the wrestling process.
- Ask for help to work through what you cannot easily understand or accept.
- Take whatever steps seem to be most appropriate as "next steps" in order to cooperate with how the Spirit is leading you at the moment.

"Yes" without limits

When you stand at the crossroads, facing the option of sticking with the familiar route or stepping onto a road filled with uncertainty and questions, but which seems to be from the Spirit, which one are you going to take? On the familiar road, you can go to church, be in a small group, volunteer, and give money, but if inwardly you know that you are holding back and that God is calling you to a greater level of faith and commitment, you are hedging your bets. Your "yes" to Christ has become a very conditional yes, almost degenerating to a "maybe."

It might be fairly easy to succumb to your instinctive reactions and continue drifting, playing it safe, or making self-limiting or even self-defeating choices. Or, you can go the other way. You can listen to everything the Spirit has to say to you. You can go with the flow and seize the opportunities the Spirit leads you to. You can go "all in" and take your chances.

I'm alluding, of course, to the moment when gamblers decide to wager all that they have on the game at hand. They cannot possibly know for sure if they will win, but in order to be successful they must put enough money into the pot to stay in the game and enough to make winning worthwhile. And sometimes, this means going all in, risking everything on their bet.

In life, all of us are placing bets every day. We invest ourselves in a relationship, a marriage, a job, an experience, or any number of other things. With each investment, we are betting that this choice will pay off for us in one way or another—yielding more love, more money, more opportunity, more fun, more satisfaction, more meaning, more something—better than if we invested in someone or something else. With each decision, each of us is making bets related to our spiritual life, too. The more we wager on what we can get out of this life for ourselves, the less we are investing in God and in Christ's call on our lives. And vice versa.

Following Christ is not a game, to be sure, but, to use Blaise Pascal's language, living by faith does require a wager. Since none of us has ever seen God or been resurrected from the dead, we cannot know for sure that there is life after death or if faith in Christ is the key to eternal life. But we can place our bets. We may not know for sure if the Holy Spirit is really at work in our lives or how God is going to provide for our needs, but we can choose to trust and live accordingly. We can resist the temptation to slide away from God or stay stuck in the quagmire of doubt and fear, playing it safe, and keeping life comfortable.

True, one's level of commitment to knowing, loving, and serving God and following Christ is always a matter of degree. If you're reading this book, you probably already have a reasonably high level of devotion and are already giving much of yourself. I certainly did when troubling questions started stirring within me, which eventually led me to make greater sacrifices and to venture further outside of my comfort zone.

The question here is not, "Do you have faith in Christ and want to know, love, and serve God faithfully?" I'm assuming the answer to that is "yes." The relevant question is, "How far are you willing to go to keep in step with the Spirit, when the Spirit is calling to go further?" In many situations, the Spirit will force us to make a choice. We will not be able to remain neutral or passive. We will have to make decisions about going forward or staying where we are. To keep in step with the Spirit requires continuing to say "yes" to God and "no" to competing impulses and loyalties, and letting the chips fall where they may.

Living your "yes"

What about you? Are your circumstances right now forcing you to make some choices? Is the Holy Spirit calling you to stop hedging your bets and go all in—or, at least, more "in" than you have been willing to go up to this point?

[Jesus] called the crowd with his disciples, and said to them, "If any want to become my followers, let them deny themselves and take up their cross and follow me. For those who want to save their life will lose it, and those who lose their life for my sake, and for the sake of the gospel, will save it. For what will it profit them to gain the whole world and forfeit their life? Indeed, what can they give in return for their life? (Mark 8:34–37, NRSV)

Keeping in step with the Spirit does not start with "yes" and then switch to "no" (though it often works the other way around when we resist the Spirit's prompting prior to finally surrendering our will to God's). Keeping in step with the Spirit means "taking up your cross" daily to follow Jesus on a Spirit-led path, where each day is different, and where the mission and assignments emerge and evolve over time. Your job is not to figure out the master plan for your whole life, but to keep committing to "yes" as the Spirit leads from day to day.

If you are wrestling with important existential questions and looking to God for answers, the Holy Spirit is surely leading you to a deeper or fuller relationship with God. The Spirit is opening your eyes and heart, and calling you to cooperate with God's prompting. You may not have any idea where Christ may be leading you long term, but, as has been stressed throughout this book, your job is to listen and cooperate as best you can. Focus on what you can receive and do, not on what you cannot yet understand, accept, or do.

And where you don't know what to think or how to change, your best resource is the same one who brought you into this uncomfortable place—the Holy Spirit, the Spirit of Christ. This Spirit who calls you to join the sacred love flow is the same Spirit who can show you the way forward and enable you to do what Christ is calling you to do.

Surely, saying "yes" to God is not something you do once, or occasionally. Saying "yes" to God is a way of life. It's a response of the heart, a commitment of the will, an attitude of the mind, and gut conviction about the purpose of your life that is lived out over and over again, every day in a multitude of ways. Keeping in step with the Spirit defines who you are, no matter what you do.

As we increasingly embrace the call to live in the sacred love flow in a world full of suffering and need, keeping in step with the Spirit necessarily requires saying "yes" to the Spirit in every way we know how, without artificial limits. We will keep cooperating with however God may be seeking to transform us and draw us into the sacred love flow. We will keep going in our day-by-day, step-by-step walk of faith, trusting that God's grace will guide and empower us to fulfill all Christ has in mind for us to experience and to do.

Listen and cooperate. Listen and cooperate. Saying "yes" to God, one step at a time, over and over again. That's how we keep in step with the Spirit.

Your next Spirit-led steps

Now that you've reached the end of this book, don't just put it down. Do something with all you've thought, felt, and experienced by reading it.

- What is the Spirit saying to you that calls for your "yes"?
- How are you going to respond?
- What are you going to do specifically?
- What help do you need? Where will you look? Whom will you ask?
- What are your very next steps?

May our Lord Jesus Christ himself and God our Father,
who loved us and by his grace gave us eternal encouragement
and good hope, encourage your hearts and strengthen you
in every good deed and word.

2 THESSALONIANS 2:16–17

Bibliography

Ackerman, John. *Listening to God: Spiritual Formation in Congregations*. Bethesda, MD: Alban Institute, 2001.

Blackaby, Henry T., and Claude V. King. *Experiencing God: How to Live the Full Adventure of Knowing and Doing the Will of God*. Nashville: Broadman and Holman, 1994.

Blackkaby, Henry, and Richard. *Hearing God's Voice*. Nashville: Broadman & Holman, 2002.

Cepero, Helen. *Journaling as a Spiritual Practice: Encountering God Through Attentive Writing*. Downers Grove, IL: IVP, 2008.

Crabb, Larry. *Connecting. A Radical New Vision*. Nashville, TN: W Publishing Group, 1997.

de Caussade, Jean-Pierre. *The Sacrament of the Present Moment*. Translated by Kitty Muggeridge from the original text of *Self-Abandonment to Divine Providence* (1966). San Francisco: Harper & Row, 1981.

Dixon, Benjamin. *Hearing God*. Chambersburg, PA: eGenCo., 2014.

Farnham, Suzanne G., et al. *Listening Hearts: Discerning Call in Community*. Harrisburg, PA: Morehouse, 1991.

Fee, Gordon D. *God's Empowering Presence: The Holy Spirit in the Letters of Paul*. Peabody, MA: Hendrickson, 1994.

Foster, Richard J. *Celebration of Discipline: 25th Anniversary Edition*. San Francisco: HarperSanFrancisco, 1998.

————. *Prayer: Finding the Heart's True Home*. San Francisco: HarperSanFrancisco, 1992.

Geoffrion, Timothy C. *One Step at a Time: A Pilgrim's Guide to Spirit-Led Living*. Herndon, VA: Alban Institute, 2008.

————. *The Spirit-Led Leader*. Herndon, VA: Alban Institute, 2005.

————. "When Prayer Makes a Difference in Suffering." *Huffington Post* (January 3, 2010). http://www.huffingtonpost.com/rev-timothy-c-geoffrion-phd/when-prayer-makes-adiffe_b_601399.html.

Hagberg, Janet, and Robert A. Guelich. *The Critical Journey: Stages in the Life of Faith*. Dallas: Word, 1989.

Hodges, Chris. *Fresh Air: Trading Stale Spiritual Obligation for a Life-Altering, Energizing, Experience-It-Everyday Relationship with God*. Carol Stream, IL: Tyndale Momentum, 2012.

Keener, Craig S. *The Mind of the Spirit: Paul's Approach to Transformed Thinking*. Grand Rapids, MI: Baker Academic, 2016.

Law, William. *The Power of the Spirit.* Edited by Dave Hunt. Fort Washington, PA: CLC, 1971.

Lawrence, Brother. *The Practice of the Presence of God.* Various publishers in hardcover and paperback.

Levison, John R. *40 Days with the Holy Spirit.* Brewster, MA: Paraclete, 2015.

———. *Fresh Air.* Brewster, MA: Paraclete, 2012.

———. *Inspired: The Holy Spirit and the Mind of Faith.* Grand Rapids: Eerdmans, 2013.

Liebert, Elizabeth. *The Way of Discernment: Spiritual Practices for Decision Making.* Louisville: Westminster John Knox, 2008.

May, Gerald G. *Addiction and Grace: Love and Spirituality in the Healing of Addictions.* New York: HarperCollins, 1988.

———. *The Awakened Heart: Opening Yourself to the Love You Need.* San Francisco: HarperSanFrancisco, 1991.

McGee, Robert S. *Search for Significance.* Houston: Rapha, 1994.

Merton, Thomas. *Love and Living.* Edited by Naomi Burton Stone and Brother Patrick Hart. San Diego: Harvest Harcourt, 1979.

McIntosh, Mark A. *Mystical Theology: The Integration of Spirituality and Theology.* Malden, MA: Blackwell, 1998.

Mulholland, M. Robert, Jr. *The Deeper Journey: The Spirituality of Discovering Your True Self.* Downers Grove, IL: IVP, 2006.

———. *Shaped by the Word: The Power of Scripture in Spiritual Formation.* Nashville: The Upper Room, 1985.

Nouwen, Henri, et al. *Spiritual Formation: Following the Movements of the Spirit.* New York: HarperCollins, 2010.

Parham, Richella. *A Spiritual Formation Primer.* Renovaré, 2013.

Pascal, Blaise. *Pensées.* Translated by A. J. Krailsheimer. Revised edition. London: Penguin Group, 1995.

Peck, Scott. *The Road Less Traveled: A New Psychology of Love, Traditional Values and Spiritual Growth.* New York: Simon & Shuster, 1978.

Peterson, Eugene H. *Eat This Book: A Conversation in the Art of Spiritual Reading.* Grand Rapids: Eerdmans, 2006.

Prichard, Rebecca Button. *Sensing the Spirit: The Holy Spirit in Feminist Perspective.* St. Louis: Chalice, 1999.

Rohr, Richard. *Breathing Under Water: Spirituality and the Twelve Steps.* Cincinnati: St. Anthony Messenger, 2011.

———. *Eager to Love: The Alternative Way of Francis of Assisi.* Cincinnati: Franciscan Media, 2014.

———. *Richard Rohr's Daily Meditations.* Center for Action and Contemplation, 2016.

Schneiders, Sandra. "The Discipline of Christian Spirituality and Catholic Theology," in *Exploring Christian Spirituality: Essays in Honor of Sandra M. Schneiders, IHM,* edited by Bruce H. Lescher and Elizabeth Liebert, 196–212. New York: Paulist, 2006.

Shockley, Gary. *The Meandering Way: Leading by Following the Spirit.* Herndon, VA: Alban Institute, 2007.

Smith, Martin L. *The Word Is Very Near You: A Guide to Praying with Scripture.* Cambridge, MA: Cowley, 1989.

Standish, N. Graham. *Becoming a Blessed Church: Forming a Church of Spiritual Purpose, Presence, and Power.* Herndon, VA: Alban Institute, 2005.

———. *Humble Leadership: Being Radically Open to God's Guidance and Grace*. Herndon, VA: Alban Institute, 2007.

Stanley, Charles F. *The Spirit-Filled Life: Discovering the Joy of Surrendering to the Holy Spirit*. USA: Thomas Nelson, 2014.

Webber, Robert E. *The Divine Embrace: Recovering the Passionate Spiritual Life*. Grand Rapids: Baker, 2006.

Willard, Dallas. *Hearing God: Developing a Conversational Relationship with God*. Downers Grove, IL: IVP, 2012.

———. *The Spirit of the Disciplines: Understanding How God Changes Lives*. San Francisco: HarperSanFrancisco, 1988.

Young, Frances M. *Brokenness & Blessing: Towards a Biblical Spirituality*. Grand Rapids: Baker Academic, 2007.

Scripture Index

Old Testament/Hebrew Bible